Wilderness Survival

Wilderness Survival

Bernard Shanks

UNIVERSE BOOKS
New York

Except for the drawing of poison hemlock, which is by Leslie Edgington, all the illustrations and calligraphy in this book are by Betsy Johnson.

Published in the United States of America in 1980
by Universe Books
381 Park Avenue South, New York, N.Y. 10016

82 83 84 / 10 9 8 7 6 5 4 3

Printed in the United States of America

Library of Congress Cataloging in Publication Data

Shanks, Bernard
    Wilderness survival.

    Bibliography: p.
    Includes index.
    1. Wilderness survival.   I. Title.
GV200.5.S53   613.6′9   80−17508
ISBN 0−87663−343−2
ISBN 0−87663−998−8 (pbk.)

Dedicated to Michael Cole Shanks

Contents

Acknowledgments

Sincere thanks are due my former colleagues at the Renewable Natural Resources Division, University of Nevada, Reno, for their support of a wilderness survival course developed during my tenure at that campus. I also appreciate the support and tolerance of my colleagues at the Forestry and Outdoor Recreation Department, Utah State University, Logan, while I worked on this manuscript. Over the past few years, the enthusiasm for both wilderness and my survival class among many students in both Nevada and Utah was a source of encouragement.

Special thanks go to Marty Lee who cheerfully typed and retyped the manuscript. Marty and many other friends were a frequent source of moral support. Many times Randy Stutman provided advice and assistance. Betsy Johnson was especially patient in developing the illustrations used in this book. Finally, I owe a special debt of gratitude to Peg Zane Evers, whose support and assistance made this book possible. During many discouraging days she always believed it could be finished, even when I didn't.

Introduction

For over two million years, man was a hunter of wild game and a consumer of native plants. Only recently has the human race raised crops and adopted a sedentary life. Physically and mentally, the human body is the product of the demands and primitive conditions of a wilderness environment. Thousands of generations of our ancestors instinctively learned survival skills or were eliminated from the human gene pool.

Not only did early man look over a landscape and find water and shelter, two essentials for survival, but he was capable of tracking, hunting, and capturing virtually every animal, large or small, in his environment. Early men and women knew and understood their environment, when plants were edible and where to find them. Humans evolved into a species with unique wilderness abilities, having excellent senses of sight, hearing, taste, and smell. A hardy species, humans pushed into harsh wilderness throughout the world and survived.

But our urban lifestyle has eroded the ability to survive. Survival skills have not been learned. Attitudes and perceptions about survival have changed in our technological world. Today, science is considered the strongest survival tool for the human race. Yet instincts and intuitive feelings were valuable to the survival of early man. Even today some people sense danger just moments before others. Intuitively, some avoid a car accident or a slippery trail or a darkened street. If they respond to their instincts, they have a survival edge over those who ignore such messages.

Over the vast scale of human evolution, a process of selection persisted, winnowing those without the ability to resist disease, illness, or injury. In a more dramatic moment, two primitive humans may have been drinking at a water hole. One paused, hackles rising, muscles tensing, eyes and nose flaring to probe for more information. The other human continued to drink. A saber-toothed tiger sprang toward the two. One, alert with the best instincts, jumped, a fraction of a second before the other. He lived. And he reproduced and passed the instincts deep into our bones, our cells, our genes.

Today we are capable of waking these hibernating survival senses — if we try. With experience, anyone can realize that a change in weather is coming, that water is near or wildlife is close at hand. Our eyes can read the lessons of the land, as well as its beauty. The sounds of wildlands can carry as many messages as the voice of a friend. Years of living in modern environments have only withered the senses. The ability to learn still remains.

Only a few generations ago, the early fur trappers and pioneers responded to their instincts and passed survival skills from one generation to the other. Failure to learn the skills of the frontier meant injury or death. Young people watched their parents and learned the best wood for fires, how to wait out a passing storm, how to fish and hunt and be reasonably comfortable in the wildlands. The literature of the fur trappers in the Far West relates many of the survival skills mountain men found essential to living. They could start a fire with flint and steel in a storm as well as on a sunny day. They could read signs on the land for food, shelter, water, and danger. Wilderness was vibrant with both resources and information. George Frederick Ruxton wrote of the Western mountain man, "A turned leaf, a blade of grass pressed down, the uneasiness of the wild animals, the flight of birds, all are paragraphs to him written in Nature's legible hand and plainest language."

Survival education in a modern world is, at first glance, an irony. However, many individuals recognize the instability of our society. A power failure in New York is a vivid reminder that most of the conveniences, as well as the necessities of life, arise from a house of dominoes. The malfunction of one small part brings down the edifice. Survival skills are a route to individual self-confidence. In our modern world, we are divorced from the process of securing shelter, water, and food, the essentials of life. The more complex the world has become, the more some people desire a simple life. Even if simplicity is not possible, the urge for self-reliance remains. It is important to have a sense of self-preservation, even as the world grows more crowded, more urbanized, and the land more domesticated.

Today, outdoor recreationists are enjoying the remarkable wildland empire of North America. For a contrast to urban and suburban life, nearly 15 million people will put packs on their backs this year for an overnight camping trip isolated from roads and developments. Millions of others camp in roadside parks or enjoy the wildlands on day hikes, by canoe, sailboat, or kayak. Once removed from developed lands, the rain pours down, the wind blows, and the earth's great processes of change continue. Millions in the outdoors are reminded not only of the frailties of our society but of the dominance of wilderness storms, mountains, rivers, and seas. They seek the frontier that shaped the human race.

Survival education can be a historic link to the skills and independence of the pioneers. Our past comes alive in the wilderness. Survival education is one way to achieve harmony with a wild environment and to overcome culturally-induced fears of the wilderness. Understanding the natural world can bring both exhilaration and inner peace. Once wilderness is understood, the deserts bring an appreciation of the constant and primeval forces at work in nature. The sea brings a sense of awe and respect. To sense the pulsating rhythms of the tide is to touch the power of the earth and its timeless dance with the moon. When the mountains and their storms are fathomed, you gain perspective of life and frailty. The wild areas of the earth are places to learn, places to grow, not places to shun. Wilderness brings self-reliance, not apprehension or dread. To be alive in the wilderness is to study its living community, to respect the earth, and to trust in yourself.

1

Survival Attitude

First, you decide to live. Once that decision is made, survival is natural. Without the will to live, survival is nearly impossible. A desire to survive is elementary and essential. And a determination to live is easy to acquire. A will to live is simply a decision that some things are unfinished, including your life.

Yet the choice is easy not to make. In an emergency, it is often easier to give up or leave the problems of survival to others. If you are depressed or unhappy, a passive resignation to your fate is an easy choice. But remember, within the wilderness of the mind, survival is the ultimate choice. Some decide not to live. They usually die. Others decide to live and refuse to give up. These choices are not new but only hidden by the facade of a modern world.

Wilderness can take a person backward a thousand generations. Alone at night, away from roads and lights, you are returned to a primal world. Quickly the confidence of Western civilization flees. Even those with wilderness experience have moments when a wave of fear threatens to engulf them. The lure of a fire, its warmth, comfort, and security becomes vital. The shadows hold no saber-toothed tigers waiting to pounce. In our heads we know this. Why then is the shadow a threat, every sound menacing? A craving for light or fire is more than a desire. It is part of our very marrow. Instinct and generations of experience are behind our fears and insecurity. Accept the fear, build a fire and bathe in its emotional reassurance.

Imagine the contrast between a comfortable home and being plunged into a cold and dark wildland. The physical stress is obvious and serious. The emotional deprivation is critical. Frequently, it is the most shocking and difficult aspect of survival to overcome. Most people are born and raised in a world that moderates climate and weather. They live in shelters that protect them not only from cold and heat but also from sun, rain, storms, wind, and even changes in humidity. It is not surprising that exposure to extreme weather, as well as lack of food or water for even brief periods, brings with it a sensation of fear.

A scenario of difficulties arrives with the fear and emotional shock. Accidents are likely to occur. Panic that is difficult to control with companions becomes nearly impossible when you are alone. But you can break the pattern. Expect the psychological shock. Plan how you as an individual will successfully cope with it. Heed the lessons of those who have survived; read case studies and stories to understand better what others have experienced.

Some people quickly give in to fear, stress, cold, and other physical discomforts without effort, without a struggle. Others confidently look at themselves and their wilderness world and begin a process of survival. One study estimated that individuals suddenly lost or thrust into a survival situation make a decision within six hours. Essentially, that decision is to live or not to live. Those who want to live change their pattern of thinking from city to wildland. They begin to make a fire, determine what can be used as food and where water can be found. They decide to take care of themselves and not to plan on others to help.

Those who fail to shift mental processes may panic or lose control over their natural instincts and rational thinking processes. They begin a series of mistakes that result in exhaustion, injury, and sometimes death. Death comes not from hunger but from dehydration, injury, or hypothermia.

Attitude or psychological state is undoubtedly the most important element of survival. With the proper attitude almost anything is possible. Take, for example, the documented case of Pablo Valencia. He was lost for eight hot August days in the Sonoran Desert. From a survival standpoint, he did everything wrong. He traveled during the hottest part of the day and rested during the cool nights. He had no equipment and wandered erratically, covering more than a hundred miles of rugged desert country. When found, Valencia had lost over 25% of his body weight from dehydration. Most people would have died days earlier. Physiologically, he should have died. But Valencia had a family he deeply loved. Because they depended entirely on him, Valencia knew in his own mind he could not die, and he didn't.

Sometimes the desire to live is based on less honorable motives like hatred. One of the classic tales is the story of Hugh Glass, the early Western fur trapper. Horribly mauled by a grizzly bear while deep in hostile Indian country, Glass was left to die by his two companions. One companion, a young and inexperienced trapper, would eventually become well known — his name was Jim Bridger. Bridger and the other trapper left Glass unconscious, apparently fatally mauled. They knew his rifle was extremely valuable and took it. Sometime later Glass gained his senses and realized he was abandoned. Unable to walk because of his wounds, seething with hatred and a determination to kill his former partners, he crawled to a fur trading post, two hundred miles away, halfway across the present state of South Dakota. His rage kept him alive, struggling against the worst of odds. Deprived of his rifle, he substituted anger and a powerful desire for revenge. Hugh Glass lived because of that anger, although he later forgave his companions.

Love and hatred are but two emotional extremes that have moved people to do exceptional things physically and mentally. Determination to reach some life goal is also helpful. When alone, remember the important people in your life and don't let the image weaken or be lost. Consider future plans and what you will do differently at the end of the experience. Learn to grow stronger as an individual and as a product of the survival experience. It was Goethe's hypothesis that those with a destiny to fulfill were blessed. One such person was a young woman, Lauren Elder, who survived a plane crash in the Sierras a few years ago. After watching her three companions die, she decided that her life was unfinished. Although seriously injured, she hiked out of the rugged mountains to safety. She later wrote a moving book about her experience. Hers is an excellent account of harnessing the power of emotions to survive.

Although the decision to live or die is undoubtedly complex, the mind has the power to will the body to extraordinary feats. Fine equipment, good health, training, and experience all can help a person survive. But without the will to live, those lost in the wilderness will despair and quickly die. Undoubtedly, this is more difficult when alone. However, you can talk to yourself, stating positive, optimistic messages on how well you have done so far. Prayer or meditation can be helpful. The mechanism or manner of self-expression is not as important as the exercise. Alone or in a group, more than anything else, attitude is the key to survival.

In the end, the decision to survive is a private one. Although death in the wilderness can usually be avoided, some will prefer death, alone and close to the earth that nurtures. By understanding the importance of a spirit to live, you can decide your personal course of action. In our modern world, it is important to understand many complex things. But when you enter the wilderness you will often find and understand your inner self. Understanding yourself is critical to survival.

Case studies of successful survivors illustrate that certain human qualities are common to those who live. Many of those who emerge safely from a wildland crisis are stubborn. Although they may be quiet and flexible in their views, an underlying strength remains. They are stubborn, dogmatic, and determined about living. In an uncomfortable environment, they set out to control what they can. They are capable of creating activity, work, or play to prevent debilitating depression. While they may be aggressive about their plight, they are not overly aggressive toward others.

Aggression can become masochistic or sadistic. Some people

will blame themselves for getting lost, for making the decision that led to a crisis. In turn, they may drive themselves unreasonably, punish themselves and others with their aggression. Determined, yes. Stubborn, of course. Improve the conditions where possible, but not at the expense of others or yourself.

The motivation and desire to change or improve your environment must be tempered. It must be restrained with the appreciation that rest, sleep, and calmness are essential. It must be modified with the appreciation that fighting anything out of your control is futile. It is helpful to understand how to take care of yourself, both mentally and physically.

Self-confidence is an essential aid to survival. Self-esteem leads not only to a sense of worth but to a sense of self-reliance. It is healthy to regard the world as something that you can change and influence. Those who feel in charge of their lives and who live in the present do well in the wilderness. Richard Byrd, facing the Antarctic alone, wrote about the importance of having faith in one's own ability and trusting in oneself. Later, after he nearly died alone in the wilderness, Byrd recounted the lessons that he learned and stressed that not once did he give up or resign himself to his problems.

An experiment in Alaska illustrates the importance of self-concept as well as physical type. A small group of scientists was selected for a strenuous trek across the Alaskan wilderness in winter. Their physical and psychological levels were monitored daily. Interestingly, despite their scientific training, most were concerned with their physical prowess. The peer pressure to do well physically was strong even among this well-educated group. The experiment concluded that lean, wiry types were more prone to apathy. Heavier individuals, although not as physically competent initially, had a more positive attitude toward their situation after a few days. Those with the highest self-esteem withstood the strain best of all.

But individual differences and attitudes do not always fit a stereotype. That is especially true with physical ability. In many cases a person seriously injured or suffering from heart disease survived under identical conditions that killed healthy athletes. The difference is mental, not physical.

Nevertheless, one aspect of survival is physical ability. If you are healthy and are leading an active life you will have the survival edge over those who are in poor shape from a sedentary life.

While the physically-conditioned person is stronger, the major benefit is psychological. Good physical health leads to higher self-esteem.

The Alaskan survival study revaled that those who are not able to complain suffered the most. The strong, silent types, unable to express deep fears and apprehensions, experienced greater stress and had a more difficult time completing the trek. Solutions to this problem are available in a group. A conscious effort to express fears, apprehensions, and ideas verbally can benefit everyone in a survival group.

The successful survival personality has several elements that combine to enhance success. The successful pattern begins with forethought. Some preparation, mentally and materially, prior to a wilderness experience, will enhance the chances of survival. Preparation may include a survival kit, a raincoat taken on a hot sunny day, or a jacket on a clear fall morning. Preparation, anticipation, and appreciation of possible problems in the wilderness point to a self-reliant person.

Those less prepared will be openly frightened and wander about aimlessly. Their efforts will be largely futile. It goes almost without saying that no matter how well prepared someone is, he will experience several fears. To be frightened under such circumstances is normal and expected. The ability to control oneself and not panic does not mean that fear is absent. The important test is whether or not the fear dominates.

A limited amount of research has been done on the behavior of individuals under survival stress. According to one report, 10% to 25% stayed calm under the most difficult circumstances, and a panicky 10% to 25% were almost impossible to handle by their fellow victims. Most people, 50% to 75%, were in a mild state of shock. They appeared confused, relatively quiet, and under control. The people in this group were responsive and almost eager to take orders and directions from someone who was prepared. They had a desire to do tasks and work on whatever was needed by the group. With the lessening of shock, this majority group became less confused and more verbal.

At the onset of a survival epic, the successful person will not panic but weigh the situation calmly. An inventory will be made of useful, available materials as well as terrain, weather, strengths of others who may be along, possibility of rescue, and a host of other considerations. The calmness will be neither passive nor overly optimistic, but realistic and rational. Plans will be flexible, not rigid.

Adaptation has been a key to survival for all living things. With changes in rainfall, sunlight, and climate, all plants and animals must adapt or be eliminated from the gene pool. Adaptation is a key psychological element of survival during a short period as well as in a long time span. To stay alive in the wilderness, a person must adapt.

The usual food resources are not available. The person who can adapt to wild foods and other supplies is more likely to stay alive. Those who retain their bias for modern food will suffer more. Physical comfort is another concern. Many people are reluctant to adapt to dirt and unsanitary conditions. The person who can burrow into a rotten log and make it his home, both physically and psychologically, is adapting. Search and rescue personnel are often impressed with the adaptability of children. Given a new environment, children will change and adapt to take care of themselves. When wet they find a dry spot. When tired they will sleep. When cold they will find a shelter. Children are less concerned with quality as long as their needs are met. Adults can learn from children. Rigid thinking and actions in the wilderness can be fatal. To adapt is to live.

Some feel that the human race is physically weak and dependent upon culture and civilization. In reality the human animal is tough, durable, strong, and versatile. Pound for pound man is superior physically to most other animals. Man can run long distances and literally outrun a deer or a horse. Most people who are thrust into a state of mild panic without a snack find it difficult to believe that a person can survive several weeks without any food whatsoever. Not only can adults survive, they can endure this stress with little or no permanent physical problems. Throughout most of their history, humans have been hunters and gatherers. Mankind adapted to a gorging-fasting cycle of eating, in contrast to today's three meals a day. Successful survivors understand their origins and their limits. And they push back those limits, both physical and mental, in a personal crisis.

The highly successful Outward Bound schools for teenagers and young adults are founded on the idea of pushing back perceived limits. The use of a physical challenge to develop individual character has been generally successful. Researchers have measured increases in self-worth and competence as the result of a stressful wilderness experience.

Understanding personal limits represents another survival key. In their daily lives, people are seldom pressed for any understanding of their own physical and mental limits. In most cases, a person's endurance is far higher than the individual generally believes. As might be expected, those who endure a survival experience are vividly aware of their increased ability to cope and deal with daily problems. The benefits can be dramatic.

The will to survive is present in everyone to some degree or other. Some people hold onto life tenaciously. Others give up with only a flutter of effort, almost welcoming an end to the struggle. Physical size and strength have little to do with the magnitude of individual survival efforts. Modern research provides an understanding of nutritional and physical aspects of survival. Yet, the will to live — the key element in most survival histories — escapes research.

Individual survival characteristics are appreciated, if not completely understood. The dynamics of group survival is more complex and the role of the individual is sometimes submerged. Nevertheless, certain patterns and group processes frequently appear to emerge during survival ordeals. Periods of monotony or routine tasks are often followed by petty bickering. A period of nostalgic memories of food and comforts of home may create a pleasant evening around the fire. Unfortunately, it is often followed by a sense of apathy and depression that should be avoided. Some will feel that loved ones have given up and abandoned them. After a few days, most people develop a sense of rejection. This often emerges when a rescue team fails to arrive or the signs of an air search are lacking. Self-pity, over your own plight or the death or injury of another, can lead to a destructive mental state.

Monotony in a long survival experience is dangerous. Routine or dull tasks can lead to apathy and despair. Apathy is a dangerous state of mind. Monotony leads to self-isolation and to the deterioration of self-esteem so important to survival. Accordingly, monotony must be coped with and purposefully avoided. Routine tasks are important, but each day must be kept new and stimulating. An active mind is open to potential innovations and helps keep the task of survival in perspective.

A program of survival does include routine. The tasks of travel, finding food, and signaling must be attended to. Fishing, the setting of snares for food, and finding water or shelter are essential activities. Nevertheless, the essentials of survival can be accomplished without a boring or dangerously monotonous pattern.

When in a group, you must take care of your own comfort and state of mind. You must avoid panic and keep up the optimism of others. After the initial crisis is over, inventory the present situation. Make a list of physical items like food and shelter, of information on the surrounding country, of the mental and physical state of others in the party. The skills and abilities of everyone are possible resources. Review with others what is known and what is not known. Set up tasks and a structure for handling resources and problems, signals, and other essentials. Do something special to cheer yourself and others. Maintain a sense of worth and a sense of solidarity. Bring into the group those who have become passive or appear rejected. Communicate fears, hopes, and plans, and involve everyone in the process of surviving. Maintain a sense of community.

But it is always important to know yourself, your hidden fears and motivations. For survival has a curious fascination. For many who function well in a modern world the attraction of the outdoors is a primal force. It lures and challenges. Some may ask, "Without the car, the house, the corner store, the credit cards . . . what would it be like?" This curiosity can lead to backpacking and other outdoor activities or it can lead inward, to a study of history, literature, and case studies of survival. In its most extreme development, curiosity about survival can express itself in an unconscious desire for the experience. The search and rescue teams of many county sheriffs' offices will often search first for the reason behind a person's disappearance or becoming lost. Did he just quarrel? Was he emotionally upset? Had some crisis developed in his life? Frequently, a powerful situation emerged prior to the disappearance. Children often run off to establish their worth or value. Often a child finds it reassuring after a serious family quarrel to be the focus of distraught parents and searchers.

There are no guarantees for survival no matter how well trained or prepared people are. But the odds favor those who tend to be emotionally stable and sure of themselves in a variety of circumstances. They lead a healthy, active life and, to a large extent, control the circumstances of their environment. They are mentally active and in tune with their bodies. They use all of their senses and carefully investigate their surroundings. In this way, they can appreciate the wilderness and their place in it. While these traits are most important, knowledge of their wildland environment is very useful.

Those individuals who understand the plants, animals, and various elements of earth and sky, water and mountains have insights that inexperienced urban dwellers lack. Some people who camp out for the first time have been frightened by the sound of crickets, fearing that they are rattlesnakes. Fear of animals that are an almost nonexistent threat in wildland areas can lead to unreasonable panic. A curiosity about plants leads to understanding their ecology as well as their palatability. Understanding the life history of animals leads to more than a dependable food supply; it adds to the enjoyment of a wilderness.

With the will to live, and some training and experience, a lost person will be likely to survive and look back on the experience as a time of personal challenge and growth. Survival, in a world of tension and self-imposed problems, can help establish fundamental, basic priorities in life. The day-to-day worries recede and are replaced with basics.

Survival odds do not favor the injured, the passive, fearful, or listless person. Several processes may develop that are dangerous. The ability to work and concentrate on the best survival strategy may be blocked. Without self-reliance, the person in trouble may rely solely on others. Fear is normal, but in the extreme it is counterproductive. Despite injuries or other problems, the individual's strength of character is still the most important element of survival.

Tenacious will drove Sir Ernest Shackleton and his 26 men across the Antarctic wilderness for five months. It was will that kept the Australian explorer Dr. Douglas Mawson going more than three hundred miles to safety. And it was the failure of Robert Scott's will, 11 miles from a ton of supplies, that caused his death in the Antarctic. Throughout the epic accounts of human exploration, during times of war and famine, the will to live has been a key to survival. Sailors lost at sea, fur trappers, pioneers, and modern hikers have had their lives measured in a test of will. Fate and luck have tipped the scales in many survival epics, but the strength of human will and the imagination of the human mind remain supreme.

2

Shelters

Winter storms on the Great Plains presented one of the most severe survival problems to pioneers. With few trees or natural barriers, the wind quickly robs the body of its vital heat. The extreme cold, combined with wind chill, could kill the hearty pioneers in a matter of hours, unless shelter was found. Even deep snow, an excellent shelter, was unavailable. But pioneers were known to shoot and eviscerate a buffalo, climb into the carcass, and weather the foulest storm. If they were desperate, they might do the same with their horses, cattle, or oxen.

To look at a buffalo and see a haven from a winter storm is an example of the imaginative thinking required when seeking emergency shelter. After a person has overcome psychological barriers to survival, shelter is the next consideration. Protection is usually needed from storms, rain, or snow. But a shelter may also be needed to keep out the sun, wind, or insects. Often the most essential need is a refuge from the fearful night.

In its simplest form a shelter is anything that protects one's body. The best known shelter is your home; however, a car, the shirt on your back, a piece of plastic also can serve as a shelter. Not only can an animal's carcass become a shelter, but also trees, logs, caves, bark, and even lowly sagebrush. Weather and terrain dictate the type of shelter, but the natural resources available limit possibilities. More often, imagination or preference limits a person's shelter. Popular conventions about blood, dirt, or smells should not limit emergency protection. The limit must be necessity, not nicety.

In deciding what sort of shelter is needed, you should go through a series of steps — a problem-solving series. The first step will be to determine what type of protection is needed. Is a storm approaching? Is shelter from wind or rain or snow required? Or is defense needed from the sun or from insects? You may also need a shelter as a psychological niche. A secure lair can reduce fears and may be needed to rest, sleep or heal wounds — mental or physical.

Another thing to consider is shelter construction. With the materials available, how much time and energy will be needed? If the ideal protection isn't available, use imagination to devise a substitute. Brainstorm a solution by considering anything and everything. Devise a shelter — even a temporary one — as soon as possible. Satisfy immediate needs first. Later it will be possible to make modifications or improvements and to experiment with other materials. But minimal shelter, in as short a time as possible, is an essential first step. Don't wait for darkness or assistance.

A good exercise for anyone traveling in the out-of-doors, through any wilderness area, would be to constantly inventory the shelter materials available Are hollow logs, brush, or heavy grass accessible? Limestone formations and many lava flows lend themselves to the production of caves, and these, of course, in an emergency, can provide protection. Also inventory the materials in a backpack or in an auto, plane, or ship. Is a piece of plastic or a ground cloth on hand? What about an extra sweater or a down coat? Any of these can serve as shelters. Is cord, wire, or fishing line available to be used in construction? No matter what the environment or conditions — desert or mountains, plains or snow — consider possible shelters while on a pleasant outdoor trip before an emergency develops.

In desert or plains regions you may need protection from the sun or wind. Carry a roll of linen cord or fishing line. Tie bunches of grass, reeds, dried brush, or several bushes together into a small hut shape. Cut or break off any unnecessary branches. In some places you can tie or weave together several flexible branches into a cone-shaped frame to hold the grass bunches. If it is warm, tie the grass bunches into the top of the frame to shade the shelter, and leave the sides open for ventilation. If it is windy or cool, tie the grass down to the sides as well as to the top of the frame. Keep adding grass until the hut is snug. Save one bundle for the door. The completed grass or brush hut should only be large enough for you to crawl into for comfort during cool weather.

In Europe, early men and women shared the same ecological niche as the giant cave bear. Undoubtedly, they approached a new cave shelter with caution. The cave bear is now extinct, but the possible hazards must be considered when developing a shelter. In the mountains, the talus slope with fresh rock may indicate a hazard from falling rock. Discolored snow, signs of rock and trees swept down, or steep brushy slopes may be an indication of hazardous avalanche areas. Certain plants and vegetation may indicate a swamp or marshy area to avoid. Camping areas with dead trees and snags in close proximity may be perfectly safe on a calm day, but those who take shelter during a windstorm risk the hazard of falling trees. A dry stream bed (arroyo or wash) in desert areas may be a comfortable place to lay out a sleeping bag, with the sand and gravel relatively smooth and comfortable compared to the coarse, desert land. Yet in a flash flood, desert stream beds can rapidly fill with water, sometimes from storms at a great distance.

Many other threats may be present. A lone tree in the middle of the meadow may be a good shelter from rain, but if there is lightning, it may be the most hazardous place to take shelter. The same holds true for a ridgetop or a damp cave immediately below a ridge. In looking for a shelter, consider not only the resources available, but the potential hazard too.

Later, after a temporary shelter is completed, begin to consider other things that complement a shelter. Is water close at hand? How readily available is it? Is there firewood? Is there a protected area for a shelter that will keep out the wind and the storm without a great deal of construction or effort? Is the refuge close to an open meadow or a place where one could signal aircraft?

A campsite and shelter will often include a fire. Might the fire spread and get out of control? Is there room to move around the fire comfortably? Is the campsite dry? Is it located high enough above a stream that the ground is not damp or moist? Will it be flooded out? Is it high enough so that you can avoid not only flash floods but perhaps an unexpected rise in tide or in stream flow? A campsite may need to be sheltered from the wind, the rain, or the sun. Take into consideration where the sun comes up in the morning and where it will be strongest in the late afternoon. Also consider whether to maximize or minimize the sun. In many regions of the north woods or in swampy areas where mosquitoes are a great source of discomfort, a windswept ridgetop or a place in the open where a breeze will sweep the mosquitoes away is an important consideration. Experienced archeologists look for windswept ridges and open areas for arrowheads, teepee rings, and other signs of ancient Indian camps. The elements of a good campsite remain through time, the same for early man and today's backpacker.

There are environmental considerations — things to consider in terms of microclimate and slight changes in the weather — that can make the difference between a comfortable night and an uncomfortable one. Both day and nighttime temperature extremes are found closest to the ground. In the desert regions, the hottest temperatures are on the ground surface. A campsite that is even a foot above the desert floor will be much cooler. The opposite is true in terms of cold. The coldest spots are at the bottom of canyons. A warmer site will be partway up a slope. Instead of camping at the bottom of a stream, move up to a bench. Don't stay next to a lake; move back from the water and above it, if possible. A valley bottom, even in the summer, will be 10° – 15°F colder than a bench a short distance up a slope. Cold night winds sweeping down a canyon or valley will add to your discomfort.

If you are close to an ocean or a large lake, consider the direction in which the land and sea breezes blow. At night, land cools quickly, and the wind blows from land to ocean. During the day the air over the land heats up quickly, and wind blows from ocean to land. This is a fairly regular pattern most of the year in coastal areas. You may want to maximize the daytime or night-time breeze or minimize one or the other, depending on weather conditions. A similar shift in winds takes place in mountain regions. The air above mountain slopes heats more rapidly than the valleys. During the day, winds tend to flow uphill. Late in the afternoon, when the mountain slopes become shadowed and cool, the wind reverses, sometimes quite suddenly, and blows downhill from mountain tops into valley bottoms. Winds flow down the same drainage patterns as water. Therefore, the best campsite in the mountains is the one that minimizes these nighttime mountain winds. Camp on flat ridges, away from streams or near the warmer middle one-third of a mountain slope, for a more comfortable night.

Local winds have fascinated travelers throughout the world. One was Mark Twain, who wrote about a diurnal wind — locally called the Washoe Zephyr — on the east side of the Sierras that, in its turbulence, would blow not just light objects and papers, but cows and horses. An exaggeration, yes, but an old example of an uncomfortable wind pattern that can be experienced almost any evening on the eastern slopes of the Sierras.

Consider some of the other climatic influences on a campsite or shelter site. Cloudy nights are much warmer than clear nights. The clouds act as an insulating blanket to keep the warm air locked into the earth. A clear night in the mountains or the desert is much colder. The temperature difference between the desert sun during the day and on clear nights is often extreme.

Clouds also affect snow conditions. On a cloudy day, snow is warmed. It absorbs more ultraviolet radiation, melts, and becomes more moist. The snow pack is excellent for making snow shelters. On a clear day, the snow is often cold and radiant with crystals. Under these conditions, it is nearly impossible to make a snowball, let alone create a snow shelter. After snow is blown or shifted, its crystals break off and the surface loses some of its former sheen. Often the drifting snow can be carved like pieces of cake into blocks for windbreaks or other shelters. Snow comes in many shapes, forms, and textures. Understanding snow and its many characteristics is part of understanding and building winter shelters.

Climatic changes influence not only snow but the air itself. Many mountain valleys during the winter months have inversions; the colder air on the valley floor is trapped by warmer air above. Sometimes the inversion causes pollution to collect in valleys, an affliction of modern urban life. The temperature change at the inversion boundary can be dramatic. You can climb a mountain slope and suddenly cross the inversion boundary into air that is 20°F or more degrees warmer. Downhill skiers sometimes experience this temperature change. They may ride the chairlift out of the cold air into the warm layer above. Skiing down into the colder air is a dramatic change and an obvious lesson on the best place to locate a shelter.

Understanding microclimatic variations can lead to modifying a shelter and its location. Even clothing design should reflect the fact that heat rises and cold air sinks. Clothing can be an essential element of winter protection. A parka with a hood on it prevents the rising convection heat, and is much warmer than a parka without a hood. People who have lived in the desert for generations tend to wear light-colored clothing instead of darker colors for the simple reason that light-colored material, reflecting part of the sun's rays, keeps one cooler. Desert people wear long, loose-fitting clothes, because skin exposed to dry air and sunlight results in a rapid loss of water. Clothing serves to keep the body cooler by keeping moisture trapped and working to cool the skin.

Winter snow, cold and wet, appears to be the nemesis of a good shelter. Yet, the Eskimos learned to survive the windswept arctic storms by embracing the snow itself. A snow cave or tunnel is often the best winter haven. In arctic conditions, with temperatures at −30°F (−35°C) and in a wind of 25 mph, exposed skin can freeze within 30 seconds. Obviously a shelter is needed in such extreme conditions. Snow is an excellent material for a winter shelter. A snow cave is much warmer and quieter than a tent. Snow is an excellent insulator. It is also a material readily available during winter conditions. Snow shelters can range from a very narrow survival niche, only as large as a bunk, to multiple-room dwellings where skiers and others can live in relative comfort through the wildest of winter storms.

Snow at first seems like an inhospitable environment for a shelter, but under very cold conditions — conditions well below freezing — snow is much warmer than outside temperatures. Because it is such a good insulator, it retains the body heat. One candle in a small snow cave can raise the temperature of the cave 10°F, and a small can of Sterno can raise the temperature 25° – 30°F. But the protection from wind chill is the most desirable advantage of a snow cave.

The arctic explorer Vilhjalmur Stefansson once recorded temperatures of −45°F (−43°C) at a snow shelter entrance. He then did a series of measurements and found temperature gradients of 0°F (18°C) on the floor and 60°F (15°C) at the ceiling. A difference in temperature of 105°F (58°C) was the result of warming the inside of a snow shelter by a cooking stove and body heat.

Eskimos who have learned to survive in the cold and snowy Arctic have more than twenty words for snow. Snow is not nearly as simple as the four-letter word implies. It is a complex material. Light, fluffy snow, with complex star patterns, begins to change even before it strikes the ground. Snow has a life cycle that brings about changes almost constantly, according to temperature, humidity, and other conditions. From the time a snowflake is created in the winter sky, until it melts under the summer sun, it evolves. Sharp beautiful crystals are broken off or melt, and the snowflakes become consolidated, slowly evolving into tight kernels. Under some conditions, the evolution of snow will create avalanche dangers. Not only will moisture or wind bring about snow evolution, but so will movement. A drift of snow is much more tightly compact — it holds together and makes a better snow shelter than snow that has not moved. On a cold winter day, pick up a handful of snow. Drop it down on the ground without packing or compressing it. A little while later you will find that the clump of snow that was picked up and merely dropped will be much harder than the surrounding snow that was untouched. Drifting snow hardens into slabs that make good shelters. The final evolution of snow, if it doesn't melt, is ice. Winter winds may cast blocks of ice upon a frozen beach,

Mat of insulating material

Snowblocks cut from trench

Snow Trench Shelter

available for shelter. Because ice does not permit the passage of air, shelters made from it must have two or more vents to assure circulation. With an ice shelter, most cracks can be sealed with snow, but some must be left open.

A snow trench is the easiest and fastest shelter to construct. It can be constructed almost anywhere there is sufficient snow, and normally it would be considered a temporary or emergency shelter. Essentially a burrow, only about 6 or 7 feet (about 2 meters) long and 3 feet (1 meter) wide, it is lined with branches or insulation to permit you to lie down on the snow. If you had a tool to cut blocks of snow, a trench could be constructed by cutting out a slit in the snow. Two blocks are arranged to make the sides and roof. They form a teepee over the trench much like roof beams. On the lee side of a log or at the base of a tree it is sometimes possible to stamp a trench less than 3 feet deep. Line the trench with branches for insulation. Cover the trench with branches, pine boughs, plastic, or a tarp, if available, to make a roof. Then kick or shovel snow over the roof for insulation, thus creating a burrow. Ideally, the entrance should be at a right angle to the prevailing wind. If the wind blows directly into the entrance, it can fill with snow. If it is blowing in the opposite direction of the entrance, snow can drift into the lee side of the snow shelter.

It is a good idea to take a pole or a ski pole into the shelter and to use it to keep the air hole open during the night or during a storm. Body heat alone will soon warm up a small shelter to 32°F (0°C). The smaller the shelter, of course, the warmer it will be. A large spacious snow cave, of course, cannot be heated as high.

A snow trench is usually too confining to cook in, and it is impossible to have a fire in it. It is essentially just an emergency shelter, something in which to weather a storm, a shelter to protect you from a cold night until you can build a more adequate dwelling or until you can hike or ski out of the wilderness area.

A snow cave is a more elaborate shelter. It may take two or more hours to build, depending upon snow conditions and the equipment available. You can dig out a shelter by hand — but that takes a lot of time and consumes more energy. It is far better to improvise some sort of tool to make the digging easier. Cross-country skiers and snowshoers often carry a lightweight aluminum snow shovel with which to construct a snow cave. You can also use a stick, or the end of a ski, if you take care not to break it. In any case, it is best to wear lightweight clothing while constructing a snow cave. Take off heavier clothes in winter conditions so they will stay dry. Clothing wet from excessive sweating can be just as uncomfortable or even as fatal as a fall into a cold mountain stream.

The first thing is to look for a place to build a snow shelter or cave. A snowdrift is the best place. Make sure that you don't start into the snowdrift only to be blocked by an obstruction. Before you start digging, probe for rocks or trees or even ice. High drifts are best — the snow is firm and well packed. Dig inward and upward. It is often possible to construct a large cave. The entrance should be lower than the shelter itself, thus preventing the relatively warm air in the cave from escaping. If the entrance is above floor level, heat in the cave will tend to rise and go out the entrance. The hole should be about 3 feet wide by 4 feet high. Once the snow cave is completed, use a block of snow or extra clothing to close the entrance during the night or during stormy conditions.

Work at a slow steady pace, and take off any extra clothes to minimize the sweating. Once a large hole is carved out, suitable for the size of the group, carve out benches to sleep on. Sleeping on a bench elevated from the floor of the cave and insulated with a pad or pine boughs will be warmer than sleeping on the floor of the cave.

The cave should have an air vent 3 to 4 inches across, preferably above the stove. A stick or ski pole should be used to keep the vent clear. If possible, dig the snow cave down to ground level, because the exposed ground has its own built-in heat supply. People are surprised to find thawed ground when they dig to the base of a thick blanket of snow, even in the coldest of winters. Snow insulates the ground and permits inherent heat in the earth to warm the soil. Even a low-level heat, roughly 32°F (0°C), will assist in keeping a cave warm. Smooth out the ceilings and sides of the cave to help keep moisture and water from dripping on sleeping bags and clothing. If dripping becomes excessive from melted snow, the roof of the cave is probably too thick, so smooth out and thin the roof to get rid of extra moisture. It also helps to poke another hole or two in the roof of the snow cave to allow heat and moisture to escape. If, after a cold night, the roof of the cave is frosted, then it is probably too thin and will need more snow piled on.

If, after a day or two, an ice glaze develops on the roof, scrape it off, permitting the cave to "breathe." This will prevent the air from becoming stuffy and carbon monoxide from building up.

It is not uncommon for the roof of a snow cave to settle as much as several inches, and this may require carving out more head room. But, it is unusual for a snow cave to collapse. As long as an arched ceiling carved out of a snowdrift exists, the possibility of collapse is relatively small. The sagging, a result of the plastic nature of snow, is a normal response to gravity.

Usually the dripping of water is the biggest problem in a snow cave, particularly if several people are staying for more than a day. To avoid the moisture, cook away from the cave itself or at the entrance of the cave with the hole unblocked.

Ironically, a snow cave is most comfortable when it is extremely cold. If the weather should turn warm, or if there should be a warm winter chinook, excessive heat and moisture within the cave may cause discomfort. So the best snow cave is made during intensely cold conditions.

Limits on the size, shape, and comfort of a cave will depend upon the depth of the snow, its hardness, the tools, and your energy. As with other survival skills, you should try to build a snow cave under comfortable conditions with adequate food. Then, if an emergency arrives, you will be confident that you can build one under extreme conditions.

Snow caves are fun to camp in and lend themselves to elaboration. Try adding grottos, extra rooms, or an indoor privy to a snowy home. Practice building snow caves and shelters with friends. Spend a cold winter night, light a candle or two, and enjoy your temporary wilderness home.

A few people have a feeling of claustrophobia in a snow cave. Some fear that it will collapse or they may suffer from breathing problems. Experience will help avoid some of these feelings. Snow is rich in oxygen, even under several feet, and carbon monoxide poisoning is usually not a serious threat. Always take a shovel or other tool into the cave. Then, even if the cave is buried under several feet of fresh snow, exit will be easier.

An igloo made of snow blocks can be a good shelter, but only under the most ideal snow conditions. To construct an igloo, packed snow and an adequate tool to cut the blocks are essential. It takes considerable skill to get the last ceiling keystones into place without having the whole thing collapse. An igloo can be fun to practice constructing, but, in most snow conditions, it is difficult to build. Proper snow conditions may be found on only a few occasions during a typical winter. An igloo is not something to build under emergency conditions, unless you have a good deal of skill and confidence. A shelter built in half an hour or even less is desired most in an emergency. A burrow at the base of a tree or under a log is much more suitable to a survival situation than an igloo.

There are several other helpful hints for living in a snow trench or a snow cave. One of the most important lessons is to take all your equipment into the cave. It can be embarrassing to go out in the morning after a fresh snowfall, not be able to find skis, snowshoes, or other equipment, and thrash around in the fresh snow in a mild state of panic looking for such gear. Once it is inside, organize and store your gear. Keep everything in its place. Stay organized and don't lose mittens, knives, matches, compass, or any vital equipment in the loose snow. Every morning and every night before getting in your sleeping bag, if you have one, turn it inside out and beat out the frost. Make sure it is fluffed up to its maximum loft and kept dry during the day.

Don't let candles or Sterno burn through the night. Candles should not be essential to staying warm in a shelter or sleeping bag. A fire may deplete the oxygen, make the cave stuffy, and add to the problems of dripping water or ice on the inside of the cave. Finally, if you plan to return when traveling from a shelter, be sure to mark the cave well. Attach a brightly colored marker on a pole or a tree. A snow cave can be quite difficult to find once you are outside. Within a hundred yards, a snow cave can disappear into the winter whiteness and leave you frightened and confused.

The basic purpose of any shelter should be to keep its occupant dry and out of the wind, heat, and cold. If nothing else, burrow into the loose soil or into pine needles or leaves. Find a hollow log or make a shelter with numerous strips of bark. If none of these are available, then try to build a more specialized shelter. The simplest, the lean-to, is useful as a temporary summer shelter. If sturdy, it may also be suitable for cold weather. In designing a lean-to, keep in mind the prevailing night wind. Understand the wind patterns in the area in order to orient the shelter to provide the maximum protection. Ideally, the shelter should be three-sided so it has an opening on the side where a fire can be built. The other three sides and the roof protect you from wind, cold, or the sun.

Depending on the geology of an area, limestone outcroppings or volcanic rock may provide caves that can serve as shelters. Many of these caves were used for thousands of years by primal men and women. Remains of these people can still be found in overhanging cliffs and limestone caves. Often, with little effort, a cave can become a first-class emergency shelter. Caves or overhanging cliffs may need a windbreak or other barrier to keep out the wind chill. In some cases, you can pile up flat rocks and make a wall, or weave thatchings. Piling grass across the entrance will make the cave more comfortable. If you are caught out in cold weather, find a rock shelter or a cave that faces south, if possible, to catch the sun's warmth. Look for one that is relatively dry. Consider the size also — one with space adequate to accommodate you and yet not so grand that it cannot be heated with a small fire or by body heat.

A fire of any kind in a tight shelter presents a deadly problem. Alone in the Antarctic, it nearly killed Byrd. It was a deadly hazard to early explorers and remains a threat in the most modern and expensive camper. Carbon monoxide poisoning results from a colorless, odorless, and tasteless gas. A product of incomplete combustion, it is a deadly possibility wherever a fire or engine is confined.

Carbon monoxide has a strong affinity for the blood's hemoglobin. The blood will absorb carbon monoxide two hundred to three hundred times as fast as it does oxygen. Thus a small amount of the poison is quickly taken up by the body. There it breaks down the hemoglobin's ability to absorb oxygen and starves the body. Yet, despite the shortage of oxygen, the body will not stimulate the normal signals of oxygen shortage. A victim of carbon monoxide poisoning will not be short of breath or have the bluish discoloration of the skin that is typical of cyanosis. The lips and fingernails will be red, not blue.

The famous arctic explorer Vilhjalmur Stefansson once found an old snow shelter in which to spend the night with two friends. Because the shelter was old and iced over, carbon monoxide from the stove accumulated. One of Stefansson's companions passed out without warning — in the middle of a sentence. The other two men, weakened and dazed, were barely able to crawl out into the cold and fresh air with their companion.

Fainting and collapse are often the first visible signs of the poisoning. Later, nausea and severe, throbbing frontal headaches may occur, and frequently they are worse when the person lies down than when he is upright. Decreased mental capacity, sometimes brain damage, may result. Because of the method by which the carbon monoxide attacks the hemoglobin, several hours of fresh air are needed to reduce the problem. Depending on the level of exposure, up to four hours in fresh air may reduce the carbon monoxide in the blood only by half. Oxygen, if available, speeds up recovery time and minimizes brain damage.

A common misconception about carbon monoxide concerns ventilation. One window or opening in a shelter is often insufficient. Depending on wind conditions and conditions in the shelter, cross ventilation is needed to assure fresh air. Some campers have used catalytic heaters, charcoal, or small gas stoves in their camper, only to wake up with a tremendous headache. Others have never wakened.

Some believe that a flame will burn low or with a yellow flame and warn of the presence of the gas. Because of the small amounts that are capable of poisoning the system, this method is not reliable. Serious damage may occur long before the flame goes out. Many Arctic expeditions have been victimized by the gas. Willem Barents's expedition, as early as 1596, suffered from the unseen foe. It nearly killed several members of A.W. Greeley's ill-fated expedition in 1884 and weakened the entire group. An awareness of carbon monoxide is one consideration of a good shelter.

A good shelter, without problems of carbon monoxide, is the wickiup, a teepee-shaped lean-to that was quite commonly built by Indians throughout the Rocky Mountain West. Loose poles and dried sticks are stacked to form a teepee or cone shape. Over this loose frame, an outside layer of grass or leaves, perhaps reeds from a marsh or a meadow, even bark or animal skins, can be placed to protect the occupants from wind or rain. Pine boughs, even dirt, are piled up on the outside. They are quite comfortable and take only a short time to build. Indians often built them for a one-night stand. With practice, anyone can learn to construct one.

A wattle-work shelter is another Indian creation. Basically, a frame of sticks is woven together. Then grass or moss or similar insulating material is piled between two parallel rows of sticks. This creates a heavy insulated barrier against the wind. A lean-to or a rock shelter can incorporate a wattle-work barrier into one wall or as a part of its design. As with most shelters, it is important to achieve comfort when sleeping. A bed of pine boughs, sagebrush bark, reeds, cattail stocks or dried grass — whatever is readily available — can be utilized for a mattress. Even in the winter, dry grass can be found around the base of trees or on south-facing slopes, where the sun has melted away the surface snow. Even if there is a great deal of snow, dry materials are still available on trees, in caves, and elsewhere, if one is imaginative in looking for them.

It is possible to make a bed that is warm on even the coldest nights. On a flat, level spot build a fairly large fire that will last for several hours. After the fire has cooled down, carefully take a couple of sticks and remove all the embers and coals from the fire bed. Cover the bed with dry, loose soil to the depth of several inches and sleep on top of it. Obviously, make sure all embers and coals have been removed, for even after several hours it could burn holes in the bedding. Even though such a bed may sound very grubby and even dangerous to sleep on, it can be quite comfortable. Firefighters have learned this technique from spending a cold night on the perimeter of a large forest fire. The most comfortable place to sit or even sleep is an area where the fire has burned and warmed the ground. With a little care, one can sit or even sleep for several hours with a great deal of comfort as heat rises from the warm ground. This practice can be used when bedding or a sleeping bag is unavailable.

Sometimes the wreckage of a car, an airplane, or some other metal hull is available for a shelter and may provide many other useful items. Metal is an excellent conductor of heat and cold, and under moderate conditions, such a shelter may be adequate. Under extreme heat or cold, however, abandon a car or plane wreckage to find a more comfortable shelter. Incorporate some of the useful items from the wreckage into a snow or rock cave or other type of primitive shelter.

Practice building several types of shelters. Become comfortable going into a wilderness area with only a minimum amount of equipment. The next step is to learn and take note of subtle differences in air temperature and air movement, and to understand the microclimate of the outdoors. A perceptive person can identify plants as indicators of warm and cold sites. Birches like cool, moist sites, cactus like warm and dry locations, and many lilies like moist riparian areas. Alpine fir prefer northern slopes as well as cool sites, and many types of plants in the composite family, such as sunflowers, are usually found in sunny and dry areas. Depending on the circumstances, those indicator plants can be signposts to guide shelter construction. As with wilderness survival, curiosity about one's environment, the outdoors, the plant and animal life, as well as the rocks and soil itself, can lead to both a greater sense of security and a greater chance of survival.

In Walter Van Tilburg Clark's classic *The Track of the Cat,*
Curt, the hunter, is caught in a winter storm. Tired, fearing the
cat and the cold, he searches for a small rock cave. He finds a
niche and quickly builds a buttress of shale rock and packs snow
into the cracks. As he blocks up the last of the entrance, he
immediately feels more secure, not only from the storm but from
the mysterious animal. He then carefully gathers some dry
twigs left by a pack rat. He gently rubs some oil from his carbine
onto the twigs and starts a small but comfortable fire. Clark's
tale may be fiction but it contains the basic elements of a shelter
and vividly describes its psychological and physical comforts.

3

Hypothermia

It killed hundreds on the *Titanic*. As old as cave man, it strikes the modern, down-clad hiker or nylon-clothed boatman. The killer is an ancient enemy of wilderness man. It first chills the body, then numbs the mind to bring death with subtle efficiency. The technical name of the killer is hypothermia and its basic weapon is cold.

Death by cold is a primeval fear. When one skis or hikes in frigid weather, apprehension grows with darkness and falling temperatures. Anyone who has faced a subfreezing night without a fire recalls the dread. The fear is based on fact. As many as 85% of wilderness deaths are caused by hypothermia. This silent, nondramatic killer with a pretentious name is far more deadly than hunger and claims more victims than animals, avalanches, or lightning.

Hypothermia has three basic tools, which usually act in concert to produce a prey. First and most important is cold. The second and third, wind and wetness, magnify the adverse effects of low temperatures and increase the possibility of hypothermia. Finally,the silent killer requires a person with low energy, weakened by a lack of food, poor health, or some trauma. Physiologically weakened, poorly clothed or sheltered, a person exposed to the three-pronged attack of cold, wind, and wetness is in trouble.

Newspapers often claim that a death in the wilderness was caused by exposure or freezing. More accurately, the victim died of hypothermia. Although widely publicized in recent years, hypothermia remains misunderstood. Fatalities do not necessarily result from extremely cold temperatures. Some wilderness hikers suffer hypothermia when temperatures are in the 32° – 50°F (0° – 10°C) range.

An example was the fate of those aboard the Greek liner *Lakonia* crossing the Atlantic on December 22, 1963. On that night a fire broke out below deck. The crew was unable to contain it, and the fire drove passengers into the water. Water temperature was 65°F (20°C) and air temperature was only slightly colder. Such temperatures are hardly extreme or stressful. But water exaggerates the cold's impact by robbing the body of its vital heat. Body cooling advances slowly under dry conditions but accelerates rapidly in damp clothing. In cool water, heat floods from the body and hypothermia develops. Before rescue, 125 of the ship's passengers died. Over 90% of the fatalities resulted from hypothermia.

Hypothermia is sometimes mistakenly attributed only to higher altitudes. But altitude in itself does not completely explain hypothermia. Although mountain tops and ridges are usually windy and exposed — prime ingredients for the onset of hypothermia — snow and rainfall are also more pronounced in mountains. Wind, cold, and moisture associated with mountains increase the risk of hypothermia as a person climbs higher.

To understand hypothermia, it is essential to understand a few fundamentals of the human body. Humans maintain a relatively constant and warm body temperature independent of the environment. In a physiological sense, people abhor cold, and much human effort and economy are devoted to protection from cold. In all climates on earth, people maintain a body temperature close to 98°F (37°C), an optimum resolved by evolution.

Other animals, such as the arctic fox, maintain a constant temperature with little difficulty. The fox is comfortable at a temperature of −58°F (−50°C). Man has much narrower limits, for shivering begins at 82°F (28°C) air temperature if a person is unprotected by clothes or shelter.

Our bodies produce heat by consuming energy in the form of food. If body temperature rises, an automatic cooling mechanism is triggered. Conversely, if the temperature falls, other protection instinctively comes into play. The most obvious is shivering, an involuntary method of warming muscles. In addition, blood changes its circulatory pattern to provide more heat for the vital organs at the body core. Circulation to extremities is reduced to save the heart, lungs, and other organs. Obviously toes, fingers, and the nose suffer first from cold and later from frostbite. The human body automatically and prudently makes this choice. If cooling continues, even the core temperature will drop. The drop in the vital core temperature — termed hypothermia — is dangerous, a threat to life.

Nutrition plays a vital part in meeting the body's requirements for fuel to maintain the core temperature. Snacks of sugar and other carbohydrates are valuable energy sources during strenuous conditions. Eat small amounts often, maintaining a steady flow of food-fuel all day long. Foods that contain protein and fat are also needed, but because the body utilizes them more slowly, their value is less immediate. Protein is more important for its staying power. For quick energy, carbohydrates are superior.

Understanding the heat-loss mechanisms leads to understanding methods to prevent hypothermia. Radiation is the most important method of heat loss. Like a radiator, the body constantly emits heat waves that diffuse into the air. A fox, with a thick winter coat, is well protected from heat loss. But humans need insulation such as clothing, a tent, or a hollow log to prevent some of the heat loss. Because of the high concentration of blood, the head is the major source of heat loss. At 40 °F (4°C), up to half of the body's heat can be lost through the head. Cooling increases rapidly as the temperature drops. At 5°F (−15°C), up to 75% of the body's heat is lost through the head. The lesson is obvious: Wearing a warm hat is an excellent way to reduce radiant heat loss. An old mountaineering maxim held the essential truth: "When your feet are cold, put on your hat."

Conduction, another method of losing heat, is the process of transmitting body heat directly into a colder medium. Unlike radiation, heat loss by conduction is usually small. Under some circumstances, however, heat loss via conduction may be important. Metal, ice, and snow all conduct heat far more rapidly than wool, wood, or similar insulated materials. Dense materials are usually efficient conductors, whereas light materials often are not. A metal zipper, nails in hiking boots, or sitting directly on snow or ice can lead to important losses of heat. Under some conditions, heat loss by conduction can be dramatic and painful — a wet tongue freezing to a tray of ice provides an instant lesson in heat conduction. Gasoline and other liquids may become supercooled and on exposed skin may produce swift, painful frostbite.

The loss of heat by conduction in cold water is even more dramatic. The thermal conductivity, or speed of transferring heat of water, is 240 times that of still air. Wet clothing, depending on conditions, can accelerate heat loss from several times to more than two hundred times as fast as dry clothing. The lesson to prevent heat loss is explicit: Dry clothing is far better than wet clothing; therefore, it is essential to stay dry if possible. Remember that clothing can get wet from sweat and overexertion as well as from rain, snow, or water.

Deaths in cold water may appear to be from drowning but in fact result from hypothermia. Boaters who fall overboard or swimmers in cold lakes may quickly lose consciousness because of the rapid loss of body heat. Although air temperatures may be high, often these deaths occur in May, June, or July, when water temperatures remain low. The cold water rapidly conducts the heat from a body. The core temperature of a swimmer may drop 6° – 8°F, with a quick loss of rational thinking. Often the victim becomes numb and nearly unconscious, then quietly slips under water.

The night of April 14, 1912, provided history's most dramatic example of hypothermia. Just before midnight, the luxury liner *Titanic* was sliced by an iceberg. Some passengers began loading into the few lifeboats available, but many boats slipped into the cold night only partly loaded. Most of the ship's passengers were left on the sinking deck. Survivors in the lifeboats were haunted by the wailing of those who floated in the freezing water. Gradually, the cries of the distress died away. One boat rowed back through the flotsam to look for survivors. Most, even in life jackets, were dead — but not drowned. A few were pulled from the water still alive, only to die during the cold hours that followed. Accounts of that grim night state that the passengers "froze," but most from the *Titanic* probably died of hypothermia. By dawn, rescue ships found the lifeboats and looked for other survivors. None were found — 1,522 people had died in the icy water.

The North Atlantic waters, which took the *Titanic* and her passengers, were cold, nearly 32°F (0°C). At such a temperature, few people survive even an hour. Studies at the University of Victoria in British Columbia illustrate the proper conduct for a person who is immersed in cold water. They estimated that survival time could be increased by one third if a person remained immobile while waiting for rescue. Researchers estimated that a person in 50°F (10°C) water could swim only about a mile before being overcome by the cold.

Studies also established that drown-proofing, a technique of conserving swimming strength by keeping the head under water except for periodic breathing, cooled the body fastest. Drown-proofing is useful for warm water, but not acceptable under cold conditions. Considerable heat is conducted from the body, especially by immersing the head. A better technique is to remain immobile, head above water, with a tightly strapped life jacket. At 50°F (10°C), staying immobile, rather than swimming, doubles survival time. Several people huddling together, with clothing and life jackets, increase survival time still more. Insulated survival clothing and life jackets are essential for long-term protection in cold water.

The most important lesson of the Canadian research is to keep the head out of cold water if possible. Swimming and vigorous efforts are futile, unless land or a boat is near. Survival time is extended if it is possible to get out of the water, even partially. The conducting ability of water makes it the swiftest tool of hypothermia. But the body loses heat by other methods besides conduction and radiation.

Cooling Power of Wind

← Wind Chill Temperature →

Temperature °C/°F

Km/hr	Knots	M.P.H.	4/40	2/35	-1/30	-4/25	-7/20	-9/15	-12/10	-15/5	-18/0	-20/-5	-23/-10	-26/-15	-29/-20	-32/-25	-34/-30	-37/-35	-40/-40	-43/-45	-46/-50	-48/-55	-51/-60
Calm	Calm	Calm	4/40	2/35	-1/30	-4/25	-7/20	-9/15	-12/10	-15/5	-18/0	-20/-5	-23/-10	-26/-15	-29/-20	-32/-25	-34/-30	-37/-35	-40/-40	-43/-45	-46/-50	-48/-55	-51/-60
8	3-6	5	2/35	-1/30	-4/25	-7/20	-9/15	-12/10	-15/5	-18/0	-20/-5	-23/-10	-26/-15	-29/-20	-32/-25	-34/-30	-37/-35	-40/-40	-43/-45	-46/-50	-48/-55	-51/-60	-54/-65
16	7-10	10	-1/30	-7/20	-9/15	-12/10	-18/0	-23/-10	-26/-15	-32/-25	-37/-35	-40/-40	-43/-45	-51/-60	-54/-65	-57/-70	-62/-75	-68/-80	-71/-90	-73/-95	-76/-100	-79/-105	-82/-110
24	11-15	15	-4/25	-9/15	-12/10	-18/0	-23/-10	-29/-20	-32/-25	-37/-35	-43/-45	-46/-50	-51/-60	-57/-70	-62/-75	-65/-85	-71/-90	-73/-100	-79/-105	-82/-110	-85/-115	-87/-120	-90/-125
32	16-19	20	-7/20	-12/10	-15/5	-23/-10	-26/-15	-32/-25	-34/-30	-40/-40	-46/-50	-51/-60	-54/-65	-59/-75	-62/-80	-68/-90	-71/-95	-76/-105	-79/-110	-82/-115	-87/-120	-90/-125	-93/-135
40	20-23	25	-9/15	-18/0	-20/-5	-26/-15	-29/-20	-37/-35	-40/-40	-43/-45	-51/-60	-54/-65	-59/-75	-62/-80	-68/-90	-71/-95	-76/-105	-79/-110	-82/-115	-87/-120	-90/-125	-93/-130	-96/-140
48	24-28	30	-12/10	-20/-5	-23/-10	-29/-20	-32/-25	-40/-40	-43/-45	-48/-55	-54/-65	-57/-70	-62/-80	-65/-85	-71/-95	-73/-100	-79/-110	-82/-115	-84/-120	-90/-130	-93/-135	-96/-140	-98/-145
56	29-32	35	-12/10	-18/0	-20/-5	-26/-15	-37/-35	-43/-45	-46/-50	-51/-60	-54/-65	-60/-75	-65/-85	-68/-90	-73/-100	-76/-105	-82/-115	-84/-120	-87/-125	-90/-130	-93/-135	-96/-145	-98/-150
64	33-36	40	-12/10	-18/0	-20/-5	-29/-20	-34/-30	-37/-35	-43/-45	-46/-50	-51/-60	-57/-70	-62/-80	-65/-85	-71/-95	-73/-100	-79/-110	-82/-115	-87/-125	-90/-130	-93/-135	-96/-145	-101/-150

Little Danger

Increasing Danger — Exposed flesh can freeze in 60 sec.

Great Danger — Exposed flesh may freeze in 30 seconds.

Convection is a third serious source of heat loss. Unlike conduction, convection heat is transferred by the motion of the air.
Convection heat loss is low when air movement is slight but
rapidly increases with air speed. Radiant heat warms the air
next to the skin, and heat loss via convection occurs if the air is
constantly swept away by wind. The practical function of clothing is to retain a layer of warmed air next to the skin. As the
wind increases, heat loss accelerates because of a wind-chill
factor. The wind chill chart illustrates the relative cooling of
wind. For example, at 0°F (−18°C), the actual temperature is
lowered an equivalent of 5°F (3°C) by a 5-mph wind. At 10 mph of
wind, the chill factor lowers the 0°F temperature to −20F
(−28°C). With 40 mph of wind, the chill factor lowers the 0°F
(−18°C) temperature to −55°F (−48°C). The solution is
obvious — wear windproof clothing or find shelter out of the
wind to avoid convective heat loss.

Wind chill can bring on hypothermia with frightening speed.
In 1969, twenty-nine school boys were enjoying a sunny spring
picnic on the slopes of Mexico's Mt. Ixtaccihuatl. Ill prepared,
they decided to climb the 17,342-feet (5,300-meter) peak. Within
an hour, they were huddled together unable to move because of a
driving snowstorm and paralyzing wind. In less than an hour
some boys became unconscious; soon after, death came. By
morning twelve were dead.

Evaporation is another source of body heat loss. When
moisture evaporates from the skin, heat is lost — a physical
process that cannot be effectively reduced. However, the
amount of sweating can be reduced and wet clothing minimized.
It is essential that moist air from sweating escape, thus reduc-
ing the possibility of damp clothing. Wet clothing loses heat by
both conduction and evaporation. Thus clothing must be able to
"breathe" to carry away body moisture efficiently. If you wear
completely waterproof clothing, water vapor cannot escape.
New synthetic materials are uniquely waterproof yet permit
body moisture to escape. Additionally, moist air can be
"pumped" out of a raincoat or other waterproof clothing by
periodically fanning the air with the clothing open. Evaporation
is often a critical problem under wet, windy conditions. Dry,
windproof, well-insulated clothing is best, although wool retains some insulative ability even when wet.

A final source of heat loss is respiration. Warm, moist air is exhaled with every breath. Under normal conditions, respiration is not a serious problem. At low temperatures and high elevations, however, heat loss via respiration can contribute to hypothermia. Elevation brings frequent, labored breath, which adds to the burden of keeping the body warm. Heat loss may be minimized by preventing heavy breathing or panting under cold conditions. Breathing through the nose rather than the mouth can also conserve body heat.

Preventing heat loss helps prevent hypothermia. The conservation of heat is therefore a major objective. But heat production is the other side of the body's energy equation. Increasing heat production helps deter or cure hypothermia. Heat is constantly generated by the human body as a result of the metabolic process. Oxygen combined with the body's fuel produces in a complicated fashion three types of heat. Basal heat production, a fixed metabolic rate essential for the minimum processes of life, is the rate of heat output for a calm, sitting person. It is partly controlled by the thyroid gland, and because it can be altered only slowly, it is ineffective in defending the body against hypothermia.

Thermoregulatory heat production is a second involuntary method to maintain the body's temperature. When the core temperature drops, even by only a degree or two, an automatic response begins. Rapid, muscular activity — shivering — commences and can increase the heat production as much as three times the basal rate. Once the body is warmed, shivering stops. However, coordination and useful movement are reduced with this method of heat production. More important, shivering consumes energy reserves wastefully. It is much better to put on extra clothing or find shelter from the cold and save the energy.

Exercise is a third method of heat production. Running at a slow pace may double heat production. Hiking uphill with a pack can produce heat at six times the basal rate. Strenuous exertion, which is possible for only a short time, can elevate heat produced by up to ten times the basal rate. The maximum, all-out effort can be sustained for approximately ten minutes by a healthy adult. Activity at five times the basal rate may be continued for an hour or two. Although this is an important way to prevent hypothermia, energy must be rationed carefully in a survival situation. Panic running or exercise will waste valuable strength. It is much better to use the energy building a shelter or gathering firewood. Otherwise, after a short, excessive period of exertion, exhaustion can result, to be followed by deadly hypothermia.

Shivering itself is not dangerous; instead it is a perfectly normal response to cold and a small drop in the core temperature. Still, it is a warning that heat loss from the body needs to be reduced. A drop in skin temperature or even frostbitten fingers and toes don't necessarily mean the development of hypothermia. It is the core temperature drop that leads to dangerous conditions. Initial shivering is a warning which indicates only the body's attempt to prevent a significant drop in core temperature. Normally it is nothing to be concerned about, unless it can't be stopped.

Shivering may continue and the body warmth may ebb because of poor physical shape, cold, wet, and wind. When the body core temperature drops to 91° – 95°F (33° – 35°C), intense shivering may result. You may have difficulty speaking or become forgetful; in general, your thinking is slowed. A brain as numb as the body is dangerous. You may not be sharp enough to perceive danger, may be uncoordinated and have an accident in rough terrain. You may be unable to start a fire or prepare a shelter. Many serious accidents occur during this early stage of hypothermia. A companion can help recognize the symptoms at this point. If alone, you must immediately concentrate on finding shelter, building a fire, and then eating.

During the next stage of hypothermia, as the core temperature drops to the 86° – 91°F (30° – 33°C) range, shivering decreases and eventually is replaced with tense, muscle rigidity. By this time, rational thinking is severely impaired. Coordination is lacking, speech almost impossible. But you may be able to walk. Failure to shiver is the best indicator of this dangerous stage of hypothermia. The tense muscles replace the uncontrolled shaking and mark the continued decline in core temperature.

As the core temperature continues to drop, the body's sophisticated mechanisms fail, one by one. While the individual response may vary according to the physiological conditions of the

Symptoms & Signs in Acute Hypothermia

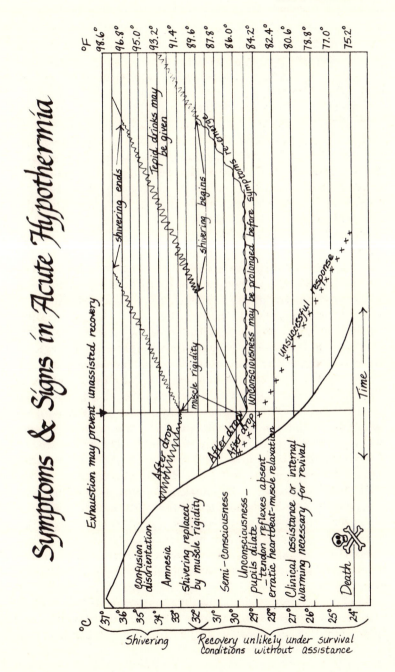

body, the general downward trend continues. The complex body chemistry begins to change. As the internal temperature drops below 86°F (30°C), serious problems develop. Pulse and respiration slow; uncoordinated, irrational behavior may be replaced by a stupor. At this point, the process of hypothermia may be accelerating as the body exhausts its remaining energy resources. Falling body temperatures can be stopped and reversed only with assistance from others. Generally, as the core temperature falls below 80°F (27°C), deep unconsciousness will result. Reflexes may cease entirely; heartbeat may become erratic. Breathing will be difficult as the respiratory functions begin to fail. Even if external rewarming begins, the internal organs continue to cool. A process of core "afterdrop" or continued heat loss makes recovery difficult. At this point in a wilderness situation, little can be done. Clinical help or internal heating is needed. If rewarming has not stopped or reversed the process, respiration ceases somewhere around 78°F (25°C). Individuals vary in response to falling temperatures, but somewhere in this temperature range death results.

The steps of hypothermia can proceed slowly or rapidly. Hypothermia can occur in only a few minutes in water near freezing temperature. Or, depending on other conditions, the process may be spread over many hours, even over a couple of days. The rapid cooling of the body can be fatal to boaters who are immersed in cold alpine lakes or in ships that go down in cold water oceans. It can occur while one is swimming in lakes or rivers, particularly in the early summer. It is helpful to wear a life jacket that gives some protection from the cold. Without other clothing, a life jacket will not necessarily prevent hypothermia. Boaters are sometimes found floating in cold water with their heads held out of the water by a life jacket — and dead. In extremely cold conditions, only a wetsuit or other survival clothing will prevent hypothermia.

Hypothermia must be appreciated and understood as a deadly phenomenon for wilderness users. Some people have died of hypothermia yet never felt really cold. Body cooling may take hours and be unnoticed until rewarming is difficult.

A healthy young man, employed by a state fish and game department, went hunting one Thanksgiving Day. He was dressed for the cold and snow; his clothing included insulated underwear, wool hat, boots, and gloves. As he climbed a hill, he entered a small roadless area only about 5 square miles (8 square km.) in size. Within this area, it would be possible to walk in nearly any direction and cross a road in thirty minutes.

Yet that evening as it began to snow, the hunter panicked. His landmarks were obscured by snow, and he began running. His clothing became wet from sweat and lost its ability to insulate. Before the sun rose the next morning, the hunter had collapsed under a large pine tree. His body temperature dropped and he lost consciousness, kicking the pine needles and pulling himself into a ball. A week later, his frozen body was found in the fetal position. But the hunter had died long before he froze. He died of hypothermia, as a result of the cold, wet clothing. Prevention and understanding are the best defense against hypothermia.

First, prevent the conditions that lead to hypothermia. Get plenty of rest, eat well and frequently. Avoid wind or cold conditions that rob the body of its heat. Stay dry, since most of the insulating ability of clothing is lost when wet. If this is impossible, carry a windbreaker or space blanket that protects the body or wear special insulated survival gear aboard ship. It is important to understand cold and to appreciate the hazards of temperatures even in the low 50s if accompanied by wind and moisture. Always have warm and waterproof clothing to prevent severe cooling or wetness. Most important, take the time to use it.

A second defense against hypothermia, terminating exposure, may be essential if you don't have adequate clothing or protection. Stop the conditions that cause hypothermia. Sometimes the most rational person is the one who has the courage to turn back from a hike or a climb and seek shelter from a storm. The person who avoids wind, rain, or snow when he or she is not prepared is avoiding the danger of hypothermia. Although mild shivering is a natural, healthy response to cold, prolonged or violent shivering is a warning sign. Seek shelter to let your body maintain its essential normal temperature. The type of shelter or protection does not matter, as long as it works.

Although you may have a tent and sleeping bag, it is important to know when to stop. At times, the exercise of hiking with a pack or walking may be the only way to prevent hypothermia.

Wind and cold may be marginally severe. Your body's heat production may drop 50% or more when you stop and permit the core temperature to fall. Therefore, it is essential to make camp or find shelter when your body still has an energy reserve. It is important to identify the symptoms of hypothermia. Always be alert for symptoms, such as uncontrolled shivering, vague, slow, or slurred speech, which serve as a warning for you or your companions. Memory lapses, trembling hands, or unexplained stumbling or lurching may be a warning, especially under wet, cold, and windy conditions, that the core temperature has dropped and the body is beginning to fail.

Apparent exhaustion or drowsiness may be another indicator of hypothermia. The old tale that sleep is fatal in cold conditions is not entirely true. A warm, sheltered person can safely sleep in extremely cold conditions. A decline in body temperature will awaken him. However, during poor weather, drowsiness, along with other symptoms, may be ominous. To lie down and sleep in wet, windy, cold conditions without shelter will probably prove fatal.

The final defense is the ability to treat hypothermia. First and most important, when hypothermia is detected, get the victim out of the wind and rain. Any shelter will serve this purpose as long as it is dry and provides protection from wind. In a shelter, core temperature can usually be maintained. If a person is immersed in cold water, there is little that can be done, but wool clothes or a life jacket can provide some protection. Quietly maintaining a position, if possible, with the head out of the water will also prolong the process of hypothermia. Swimming or thrashing in the water only accelerates heat loss. Most desirable is to get out of the water onto a capsized boat or log.

In a wilderness situation, remove all wet clothing and replace it with dry garments, if possible. Place the person in a dry sleeping bag or space blanket, if available, and add extra heat. In severe cases, the core temperature of the body drops although the body's surface is warming. Under these conditions, the body may not be able to rewarm itself without internal warming. Heat may be added by giving the person warm drinks. A more effective technique is to boil water and have the victim carefully breathe steam, which heats the heart and lungs rapidly. This technique, called inhalation rewarming, can be done with portable specialized equipment in the field. Such equipment should be available to rescue units and those exposed to severe conditions.

Do not give alcohol. It complicates the problem of rewarming. Alcohol produces a dubious sensation of rewarming because the blood vessels near the skin surface open. Blood travels from the core where it is needed most to the skin surface, permitting the loss of vital heat needed in the core. This accelerates the after-drop process or continued cooling of the heart and lungs. Even after rewarming begins, the core will continue to cool. Despite the myth of brandy helping a chilled person, alcohol is one of the worst first-aid treatments.

In the field, other rewarming methods should be attempted. Obviously, a fire is important for heating fluids, drying clothing, and warming the victim. Any additional heat loss and temperature decline must be prevented. Placing a victim in a sleeping bag may not be sufficient. Often it may help to surround him with warm bodies. Constant attention and care are needed once he is in a warm, dry place. Some have died of hypothermia when their well-intentioned friends left them in a sleeping bag and went for help. It is more important to continue to care for the person until the body core temperature returns to normal.

Acclimatization to cold takes place within the body. As with most aspects of human physiology, the degree of adjustment to cold varies among individuals. The clothing or protection one person needs against the cold may be inadequate for someone else. The variables may be age, physical condition, or nutrition. The presence of certain vitamins and minerals may make a subtle difference within the body. Past drinking and eating behavior can also alter resistance to cold. Each individual must determine for himself what protection and shelter from cold he needs. Recognize the physical variability in yourself and others.

The human body functions best within a strictly limited temperature range. Cold is the basic weapon of hypothermia. But wetness rapidly accelerates cooling, and wind magnifies the cold dramatically. Hypothermia is best combated by prevention, proper clothing, staying warm and dry, and eating properly. If necessary, treatment must be immediate and complete. Through an understanding and respect for hypothermia, many needless deaths can be prevented.

4

Fire

Jack London captured the importance of a simple fire in his tale *To Build a Fire*. Traveling during the bitter Arctic winter, a man stops to build a fire. The terrible cold has numbed his brain as well as his hands. In desperation, he uses the entire supply of matches. As the fire builds and begins to warm and comfort him, snow cascades off the overhanging tree, burying the flames and the man's hope for survival.

A fire has many uses. As well as preventing death by hypothermia, it provides comfort and security. A fire soothes the body and returns the mind to rational and practical solutions for whatever problem has developed. Even lost or panicked, the person who can build a fire will almost surely survive. The nursing of a fire to life will in turn nurse the human body back from disaster and death.

By the light of a fire, a person will be calmed and feel secure from real or imagined animals. The light from a fire can also signal for assistance and guide companions to camp during a dark night. Three lights or fires are a standard distress signal.

Add a spare tire, green boughs, or plastic to create smoke for signaling rescuers.

A fire can lead to more than a sense of security. It can be used to dry, smoke, or preserve a variety of foods for later consumption. More useful, a warm stew, bubbling over a hot fire, will transform an astonishing collection of creatures into a palatable meal. Heat from a fire can melt snow, purify water, or sterilize a knife.

Pacific Northwest Indians used fire as a tool to hollow out logs for home construction. The same concept, using fire as a tool, can be applied today. A stick can be hardened and shaped into a weapon. Fire can burn logs into manageable lengths for shelter, traps, or other equipment. Indians used smoke from a fire to repel insects. Pioneers used smoke on beehives found in the wild; bees stunned and groggy are less apt to sting to protect their honey. Smoke can be used to drive small animals out of their burrows and into a trap. Animals can also be driven by the careful use of fires. Early man used fire to stampede animals into traps or over cliffs. A torch at night blinds fish in small streams and makes them easier to capture.

The single most important survival tool, after a person's own intellect and knowledge, is the simple match. In a wilderness setting, matches should always be carried. A hunter can start a fire with his rifle and shells. A bird watcher can use binoculars to focus the sun rays. A camper can use flashlight batteries or flint and steel. But the best, most dependable survival tool is a match. Carry matches in a waterproof container.

A fire needs three things to burn. Without any one of the three, the fire ceases to exist. First, fuel is needed. Anything that is combustible — wood, grass, coal, blubber, or oil — is fuel. Second, a fire needs air, or more specifically, oxygen. Without oxygen, a fire goes out. Finally, a fire needs heat. The exact amount of heat to start a fire depends on fuel size. A single match will ignite small sticks, steel wool, and other fine-sized fuel. But a single match won't light a log or a bar of steel.

There are three types of fuel for starting a fire. First and most important is tinder, or very fine material that is essential in igniting a fire from a small source of heat. Many kinds of tinder are available. Paper is a common one. In an emergency, use part of a map, toilet paper, or the paper wrappers left in coat pockets. Protect and hoard it, for excellent tinder is hard to find in an emergency. Pine needles, dry and protected under logs or at the base of a tree, are another source of tinder. Milkweed pods or the dry heads on cattail fronds are good tinder. Grass, moss, leaves, and other materials may be found protected in niches sheltered from the hardest rainstorm. Fine material may be found in a bird or mouse nest. Other sources of tinder may be found under rocks, in hollow logs, or sheltered in trees. Sagebrush bark and the thin bark of other shrubs are good tinder.

Tinder can also be made. You can carefully shave a dry stick with a knife to produce thin strips of tinder which mountain men call a fuzz stick. Pitch oozing from wounds in a pine tree or a pitchy piece of wood can produce tinder that is readily flammable. Even in the absence of a knife, rubbing a stick on a sharp, dry rock can shave small amounts of tinder.

Kindling, or small fuel, is the next step in the process of gathering wood for a fire. Kindling, like tinder, must be dry. Small twigs in trees are surprisingly dry even in a snowstorm. Test them. Dry kindling will snap and not bend when broken. Again, nests from certain birds and animals can provide both tinder and dry small twigs that will be useful in starting a fire. Explore the surroundings and learn where nests are. Recognize the signs of a packrat burrow going under a rock or log. Learn

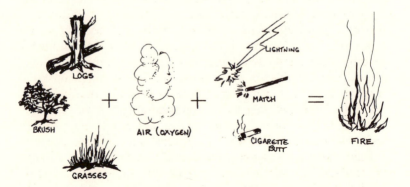

FUEL + AIR + HEAT = FIRE

to recognize pinon pine or other trees that tend to have heavy pitch.

A third category encompasses larger pieces of wood or fuel. These may be logs, pine knots found in a rotten log, seal blubber or other animal fat, or dried animal dung. Heavy fuel need not be completely dry. Break branches by hand or over rocks or logs. Gather driftwood along lakes and rivers. Dry washes in desert areas often contain dried, uprooted shrubs and small trees that provide a source of heavy fuel. Cow chips and fence posts may be found in plains or desert areas. You don't need a hand axe or hatchet for gathering heavy fuels. Wood that you can't gather by hand or break can be burned into manageable lengths.

Once your tinder, kindling, and heavy fuel are gathered, you are ready to start your fire. First, select a good site, one that is protected from wind and rain. Associated with the fire site should be a good spot for camp or a shelter, unless the fire is only for a short break or for drying out. The best site will have a rock or log for shelter from the wind and to reflect the heat back. Under dry or windy conditions, be sure the fire does not spread and create a large forest fire. Clear all brush and other burnable material away down to the soil. Don't build a fire where stumps or roots will smolder long after you're gone.

Carefully arrange tinder and other fuels so they are protected from rain, snow, and wind. Some prefer fuel arranged in teepee shapes, while others arrange it in neat stacks or a miniature rack of tinder and twigs. The exact manner of stacking or arranging fuel is not as important as protecting the fuel and arranging it compactly enough to carry a small flame. Stack a few small twigs to capture the rising heat and flame. But remember that plenty of air must be able to reach the fuel and flame. As with other survival skills, practice is the best way to learn the right balance of loose stacking of tinder and small fuel which will efficiently lead to a larger and larger fire.

Always carry extra matches in your coat, pants, and pack, as well as in waterproof containers. Specialty matches can be purchased which are relatively windproof and waterproof. Always try to start a fire with one match. If one word describes the start of a fire it is "nurture." Nurture the small flame. Light the tinder at the bottom since the flame will rise and preheat other fuel.

Gently blow on it if it appears to be smoldering from excessive fuel. Once the twigs begin to catch fire, gently add more. But don't leave the fire until it is well established. Once the fire is strong and healthy, then gather more large fuel to feed it. Winter brings its own problems with fire. Campfires built under snow-laden pine trees are easily snuffed out. A bed of green logs or rocks may be needed to keep the fire from melting into the snow.

An unexpected fall snowstorm often confuses hunters and makes a fire essential. A few years ago such a storm caught a young hunter out in the Rocky Mountains. Snow was still falling when he stumbled along a lakeshore, cold and miserable. Seeing a large fir tree emerge out of the storm, he left the shore, pushed aside the brush and fell on the needles under the tree and out of the snow. His clothes were wet, and after hours of shivering he felt only numbness from his stiff muscles. Expecting a successful hunt, the man had carried a camera but no matches. After resting, he struggled to a sitting position and slowly fired his rifle again and again into the cold wilderness night that began to surround him.

A week later, a young ranger also stumbled as he approached the lakeshore. Tired from six days of searching, he felt weary and certain the hunter was not to be found. Then he saw the rifle neatly propped against the fir, bolt open. The rest of the scene raced through his vision — the red wool coat, the black hair, and the empty shells on the ground. Slowly, he circled until he met the frozen glaze of the hunter's eyes. Then he stared again at the shells that littered the ground around the body — the key to starting a fire in the worst of storms had been wasted signaling for help.

Hunters always carry the potential material to start a fire. The powder in a shell can be broken open and poured into a small depression. A spark from a knife or any other source will ignite the powder. Once it flares, it will ignite the tinder and fuels that have been carefully prepared. Without a knife or source of spark, the powder can still be ignited. Remove the bullet and powder from a shell. Carefully pour the powder into a small depression and lightly cover it with kindling. Place the barrel of the handgun or rifle over the powder. Fire the shell, which has only the cap left in it, slightly over the top of the nest. Do not fire directly into the nest of powder and kindling or it will scatter. If successful, the blast of flame will ignite the small target. Try this technique and practice until it is perfected.

In an emergency, other methods of starting a fire may be used. If the day is sunny, a magnifying glass, broken bottle, eyeglass lens, or binocular lens may be used to focus the sun's rays on tinder. If the tinder is dry and crisp, carefully focused sun rays produce sufficient heat to start a fire. Obviously, this techique is limited to relatively good weather conditions. Try it. It is reassuring to know several ways to start a fire.

A couple of flashlight batteries and a small piece of steel wool will also start a fire. Roll the steel wool into a long thin worm. Hold the flashlight batteries together one on top of the other — the top (+) of one cell should contact the bottom (−) of the other. Place one end of the wool on the bottom of the batteries and the other end at the top. Once the circuit is complete, the heat will ignite the steel wool. If fine steel wool is used, numerous sparks will fall. These can be transferred to the kindling and used to nurture a fire. Obviously, a car battery and wire will also suffice in an emergency; just complete the circuit from the positive pole to the negative one and catch the sparks. Often a battery unable to turn over a car will still generate enough sparks to start a fire. And don't overlook a cigarette lighter as a source of heat and fire.

A knife and piece of flint can also be used to start a fire. First, find a piece of rock hard enough to knock a spark off a knife, belt buckle, or other piece of metal. It is important to knock a fairly large hot spark off with some accuracy. Ideally, it should fall into a nest of kindling that is prepared. If the kindling is dry and fine, you can blow the spark into a flame with gentle nursing. As with other techniques, practice at home, in good weather and bad, until you perfect the method. It takes time to learn the skill to direct the spark accurately into the tinder.

A common joke concerns starting a fire by rubbing two sticks together. Friction heat can ignite a spark this way, but only with the proper wood, extreme care, and nearly perfect technique. It is not recommended. Under poor conditions, it might take hours to start a fire in this manner. It is better always to carry matches in a waterproof container and render such techniques unnecessary. Starting a fire with a bow and arrow drill or using two dry sticks is possible, but under adverse conditions the method is often a futile one.

Most people cannot start a fire, even under dry conditions, with a single match. The reasons: First, they are inexperienced. Our modern world has deprived us of the daily chore of starting fires for warmth and cooking. A machine or thermostat does this simple chore for us. Like a muscle that isn't used, the skills or knowledge of how to start a fire wither away. Another common reason for failure is impatience. Many are in a hurry and fail to carefully nurture their fire and flame into a healthy fire. If they are impatient under ideal conditions, it will be impossible for them to start a fire under poor conditions. And to make things worse, most people select inferior fuels for starting a fire. Good, dry kindling is not found on the ground. It must be carefully sought after in various nooks and crannies. No attempt to start a fire should be made without the best fuels available, or matches and other means for starting a fire will be wasted.

Stefansson wrote of Eskimos' starting fires under stormy conditions using pussy willow fuzz for tinder and pyrites, or "fool's gold," for sparks. They would then warm their snow shelter with a wick stove. A wick stove can be made from any solid container. A hub cap or metal can may be used to hold oil, fat, lard, or petroleum products. A wick can be improvised from a wire twisted around a rag, an extra shoelace, or even shredded bark. After one lights and adjusts the wick, several hours of warmth can be gained from a hub cap full of oil. Control the size of the fire by the size of the wick. A wick stove can be very useful in a snow shelter.

But fire, despite its numerous benefits and advantages, is not without problems. In tents, campers, and closed areas, the greatest and most subtle danger is carbon monoxide poisoning. A charcoal burner, catalytic heater, or other unvented fire in a van or camper is potentially fatal. So is the careless use of fire or stoves in tents and shelters. Lightweight backpacking stoves can overheat and explode. Most tents and modern camping gear are made of nylon or other synthetic fibers that are flammable and dangerous around fire. At the very least, a melted hole in an expensive down sleeping bag is a sad and expensive way to learn about fire. At worst, a tent can burn and scar for life. Cook outdoors if at all possible, or at least at the entrance to the tent.

Every summer, forest fires are a danger to hikers and wilderness users. Some have suggested that if you are trapped in a forest fire you should follow animals to water holes or lakes. Unfortunately, with this advice, you might have a long hot wait until an animal dashes by on its way to water. Several rules and basic principles should be understood to cope with a forest fire.

First, fire spreads uphill much faster than downhill. Never try to outrun a forest fire by climbing a canyon or steep slope. Such areas act as natural chimneys and speedily draw the fire upward. Instead, try to work below or downhill from a fire.

A number of years ago, a large fire near Helena, Montana, was approached by a team of smokejumpers who had parachuted into the hills above the fire. They traveled downhill and began to fight the fire, but they were unable to control it. The men should have approached the fire from the flanks and kept a safe escape route. Aided by winds and the natural tendency to burn uphill, the fire spread. The smokejumpers, in excellent physical condition, began to run uphill away from the fire. A race for life began as the panting men struggled to stay ahead of the flames. One by one, the men began to drop, first the weakest, then the stronger ones. Most were killed — twelve out of sixteen — before they reached the hilltop. Most were not physically burned. They had inhaled hot gases that seared the delicate tissues in their lungs and asphyxiated them. Once trapped they should have cleared the ground of fuel and buried their faces in the cool earth to avoid the heat. The fire probably would have swept over them in just a few minutes with less devastating results.

Wind rapidly supplies oxygen to a fire and greatly enhances its spread and severity. Be conscious of the wind direction and do not run downwind from a fire. Instead, move at a right angle to the wind, if possible. The type of fuel available greatly affects its spreading power. Flash fuels such as grass, dense stands of trees, and shrubs are areas to avoid. Ridge tops with little vegetation, wet meadows, or areas near water are much safer.

Forest fires are also influenced by other factors. For example, the higher the air temperature the higher the risk of forest fires. Cold weather and cool temperatures keep fire danger lower. The opposite holds true for humidity. Low humidity means high fire danger. Damp or humid weather slows the spread of fire. If you can smell and feel dampness in the air, then the fire danger is low. Forest fires are also directed by the exposure or aspect of the terrain. Southern exposures and the middle portion of a mountain slope are the hottest and most susceptible to fire.

Specifically, what can you do if caught near a large fire? First, try to keep calm and think rationally. If in an auto, do not try to drive through a fire. Your engine may quit because of the lack of oxygen. The internal combustion engine needs the oxygen as much as a human and cannot operate without it. If it is impossible to drive to safety, leave the auto in an open area and try to escape on foot.

Check the wind direction and fuel. Avoid heavy-timbered or brushy areas. Avoid dry grassy slopes; they spread a fire rapidly. Stay as calm as possible and don't panic at the approach of flames.

If it is impossible to avoid a fire, try to find a moist area, water, or even a bare spot where fuels are not close at hand. Keep low to the ground, face down in the earth. If possible, breathe through a damp cloth or shirt. If in water, dunk your head to cool it. Roll down shirt sleeves and button up shirt collars. Sparks and hot embers are painful. Always have a safe escape route. Know at least one good path or route away from fire danger.

Forest fires are a minor survival problem under normal conditions. But remember that fires can surprise even experienced firefighters. Temperatures can reach 2650°F (1450°C). At that point, rising heat creates its own wind and storm of fire. Air is drawn into the center of the fire and the oxygen is consumed by the holocaust. A fire storm is a rare natural disaster, as unusual as a major earthquake—but just as deadly. The infamous Peshtigo fire burned in the Wisconsin woods at the same time as the great Chicago fire. On October 8, 1871, an estimated fifteen hundred people perished. A large forest fire killed more than four hundred people in the Hinckley, Minnesota, area on September 1, 1894. Even today large fires spread and threaten lives.

Alaska's forests dry out during the long summer days and

sometimes large fires result. One Fourth of July a plane load of smokejumpers parachuted into a small Alaskan fire. Winds soon spread the fire, burning fire-fighting equipment and expensive cargo, as well as many acres of forest. Two experienced jumpers attempted to salvage some needed gear. Veterans of nearly a hundred fires, they were confident that they were safe. They weren't. A fire storm was brewing and the fire broke over them with a deafening roar. Both men instinctively dove for a marshy bog. The fire burned everything around them. For a few minutes even the available oxygen was consumed by the huge fire. They panted for air, cooling each breath through their wet shirts. The fire quickly spread past them. Later, the two emerged wet, dirty, and smelling from a bog. They were very lucky to be alive and they knew it; and they had more respect for forest fires.

5

Water

Survival literature abounds with eloquent accounts of those who nearly died of thirst. Descriptions of the sweet taste of water are poignant. Late in the 19th century, explorer Sven Hedin suffered immensely from thirst in an Asian desert. He finally arrived at his goal.

> I stood on the brink of a little pool filled with fresh, cool water—beautiful water! ... I lifted the tin to my lips, calmly, slowly, deliberately, and drank, drank, drank, time after time. How delicious! What exquisite pleasure! The noblest wine pressed out of the grape, the divinest nectar ever made, was never half so sweet.

The human body is largely water, a walking water radiator. Adults are composed of 75% water, children even more. A primitive physiological mechanism normally maintains the human water balance within narrow limits. Any changes in the water balance, even less than 1% of the body's weight, brings a rapid response. The process of water balance and the role of water in the human body are complex. Although the process is complicated, the fact is simple — water is essential to human life. Deprive the body of water and survival is soon threatened. Dehydration must be understood to fully appreciate water's role.

Thirst and dehydration bring discomfort and serious physical and mental problems. Water loss must always be replaced to keep the body at an efficient level of performance. A loss of 1 to 2 quarts (liters) of water can result in a 25% loss of physical efficiency. If dehydration continues, thirst becomes unrelentingly painful. Death by thirst is a terrible fate. Death from cold, drowning, or even starvation is gentle by comparison.

The human body can be dehydrated in several ways. Air temperatures above 92°F (33°C) trigger sweating to cool the body. Water loss through sweating rises with increased temperatures, humidity, or physical activity. Under extreme conditions, well over 2.2 pounds (1 kilogram) of water can be lost each hour. With excessive sweating, 1 to 2 quarts (liters) of fluid must be consumed each hour to maintain the body fluids.

Sweating is not the only way the body loses water. Illness or disease can result in dehydration. Water loss can also be caused by lactation, urination, or hemorrhaging. Fear, dreams, and other psychic suggestions can cause dehydration or a sense of thirst. The consumption of alcohol increases dehydration. Alcohol in the body blocks the release of an antidiuretic hormone in the pituitary gland. Urination increases as a result. Coffee and certain drugs, such as those used for colds or congestion, can trigger a related response. Consequently, water is more readily lost from the body and a state of dehydration can more easily be reached. Water is lost directly from the body by vomiting and diarrhea. Some body fluid is lost by panting, especially under dry conditions. A common cause of dehydration is sunburn; considerable fluid can be lost directly through burned skin.

The consumption of certain foods, especially proteins, requires water for the process of digestion. Salty, spicy, or sweet foods also increase the demands made on the body's fluid store. During conditions of water shortage, it is better to cut back on the consumption of food to lower the body's water requirements.

The first and most essential need for water is to cool the body. Water required to cool the body cannot be conserved past a minimum point. Even at rest, the body produces approximately 80 calories of heat each hour as a basal rate. If efficiently utilized, this heat would boil nearly a quart (liter) of ice water.

For example, an average person who is out of doors under a clear sky for one hour at 100°F (38°C) will gain 150 calories of heat from the sun. Another 150 calories are gained from ground radiation. Therefore, the body must cool 80 calories of basal heat, plus 300 calories of direct and indirect solar heat. And any physical activity also increases the body's heat production. The average person who walks 3.6 miles (6 km.) in an hour produces an additional 200 calories of heat. The total heat the body must dissipate now totals 580 calories, from one hour's walk in the sun at 100°F (38°C).

The evaporation of sweat from the skin requires heat and consequently cools the body. Evaporating a cup of water or sweat will reduce body heat by 136 calories. A quart (liter) of water consumes 514 calories of heat. Therefore, the 580 calories of heat a body gains in an hour-long desert hike requires over a quart (liter) of water for cooling and maintaining a normal temperature. What was lost by sweating to cool the body must be replaced.

Usually fluid loss by sweating results in thirst. The sensation of thirst can be triggered by a fluid loss equal to 1% of the body's total weight. But the sensation of thirst is not always an index of water need. Under extreme hot and dry conditions, an adult can lose as much as 15 quarts (liters) of water in a single day. Despite serious dehydration, he may be so preoccupied with heat, sweating, and discomfort that he does not fully develop symptoms of thirst. He may also fill his stomach with water and still be dehydrated.

The loss of body fluid is a serious problem. Dehydration of 2% – 4% of the body's weight can cause an increase in heart rate and respiration. Muscle spasms and cramps can develop, and the ability to work diminishes. Dehydration commonly brings nausea and poor judgment. Thirst often causes mental instability and depression. But some people blame their symptoms on illness, disease, or weakness.

It is imperative to recognize the symptoms of dehydration in others. Wet clothes are an obvious indication of excessive sweating; another is the accumulation of salt on clothing. Look at the other person's face for red or pink skin, a sign of overheating. Sometimes a dehydrated person will withdraw from a group, slow down, or display poor coordination. He may hallucinate, be irrational, or have other indications of deteriorating judgment.

People sweat at different rates according to disease, medication, and physical condition as well as differences in physiology. Water requirements are personal and shouldn't be regulated by group needs or schedules. Personal signs of dehydration must be recognized. One good indicator is dark yellow urine. If the urine is very dark or impossible to produce, serious dehydration has occurred and must be corrected. As dehydration continues, other symptoms develop.

Dehydration equal to 5% – 10% of total body weight can result in dizziness, headaches, and tingling in the extremities. At this point some people may have difficulty breathing and speaking. Diminished body fluid thickens the blood, and circulation becomes difficult. Poor circulation results in people having difficulty tolerating heat and maintaining a normal body temperature. But if the fluid is replaced promptly, the human body can tolerate a 10% loss in body weight from dehydration without serious problems.

If the fluid is not replaced promptly, individuals may become delirious or hysterical; the tongue swells; swallowing becomes difficult, then impossible; the mouth becomes numb; the skin shrivels, and movement may be painful; vision begins to fail, and partial deafness may occur; restricted blood flow from thickened blood strains the heart. The level of pain and suffering is incredible. D.T. MacDougal, an early American botanist, reported deranged desert travelers in the Southwest, in the advanced stages of dehydration, who obliviously forded streams and wandered onto dry plains. They were crazy from thirst.

Depending on the air temperature, the speed of dehydration, and the will to live, death occurs between 15% and 25% dehydration.

The water requirement chart indicates the expected survival time based on different temperatures, water available, and two

No Walking... Resting in Shade

Max. daily temp. in shade °C.	°F.	Available water per person (liters)					
		0	1	2	4	9.5	19
49	120	2	2	2	2.5	3	4.5
43	110	3	3	3.5	4	5	7
38	100	5	5.5	6	7	9.5	13.5
32	90	7	8	9	10.5	15	23
27	80	9	10	11	13	19	29
21	70	10	11	12	14	20.5	32
16	60	10	11	12	14	21	32
10	50	10	11	12	14.5	21	32

Average days survival time

Walking at night until fatigued, then resting

Max. daily temp. in shade °C	°F	Available water per person (liters)					
		0	1	2	4	9.5	
49	120	1	2	2	2.5	3	
43	110	2	2	2.5	3	3.5	
38	100	3	3.5	3.5	4.5	5.5	
32	90	5	5.5	5.5	6.5	8	
27	80	7	7.5	8	9.5	11.5	
21	70	7.5	8	9	10.5	13.5	
16	60	8	8.5	9	11	14	
10	50	8	8.5	9	11	14	

Average days survival time

levels of activity. Individual survival times vary greatly. Drinking one or two quarts of water at high temperatures does not significantly increase survival time. Study the chart carefully to understand the need for several gallons of water when exposed to extreme desert conditions.

The chart does not illustrate survival time for daytime walking at high temperatures because survival in such conditions is stunningly short. If a healthy person started walking in 110° – 120°F (43° – 49°C) temperatures without water, he would travel only a few hours and probably less than 9 miles (15 km.). If he started in the morning he would probably be dead by sundown. If he were weak or sick he would probably collapse after a mile or two.

A person sitting quietly in the shade with 1 gallon (4 liters) of water available during 120°F (49°C) daytime temperatures will die within two and a half days. The ability to think rationally and more efficiently wanes much faster. Obviously any travel under such conditions is dictated by the consideration of water. Under conditions of dehydration all of a person's ingenuity must be directed toward finding water and preventing further dehydration.

Considering the great potential for dehydration, how do you cope with this dreadful prospect? Many old army field manuals insisted that restricting water consumption must become a habit. That is wrong. To operate efficiently, you should drink water whenever you are thirsty. Even if water is in short supply, survival time can be lengthened by drinking what water is available, rather than rationing the supply. Some desert travelers have died with rationed water in their canteens.

It is possible to "tank up" with water prior to leaving a water source. A quart or more of water can be held in the stomach. An additional quart or more can be accumulated in body tissue by sustained drinking prior to departing on a hike or trip. This will extend your range of travel and survival time.

During hot weather it is advisable to carry 5 gallons (20 liters) of water per person, per day. Usually the weight of water is not a serious problem for a car or boat. However, substantial amounts of water can't be packed by hikers and backpackers. If travel is planned in desert areas, it must be carefully planned around water supplies.

If time is available, it is possible to condition the body to utilize water more efficiently. In two or three weeks, by a complex process of adjustment, the body becomes acclimatized to greater heat. Prior to a trip, spend several days in the sun. Avoid air-conditioned buildings and automobiles. Good physical condition also aids in the efficient utilization of body fluids. After acclimatization, the body is more efficient, sweats less, and utilizes water frugally.

Even more important is the conservation of body fluid. There are several ways to reduce consumption of water. Don't travel during the heat of the day unless you have very large amounts of water and the ability to carry it. Dehydration increases several times faster when you walk under the desert sun. You are much better off to travel after 6 o'clock in the evening — even at night, if there is sufficient moonlight or if a flashlight is available — and before 10 o'clock in the morning. Find shade or construct some sort of shelter in which to rest during the heat of the day.

Another general rule is to ration sweat. Bare skin or a bare head exposed to the sun requires substantially more water to keep cool. A loose-fitting shirt can more efficiently use sweat for cooling and result in significantly less drain upon the body's water supply. Because of the many blood vessels in the head, it is particularly susceptible to the sun's overheating. A hat will keep it cooler and more comfortable. The color of your clothing is also important. Light-colored or white clothing will reflect a significant amount of sunlight and heat. Dark clothing absorbs the heat. Loose-fitting, light-colored clothing is far superior to dark, tight clothing.

To travel or not to travel, for example, from a plane crash or a disabled auto, is literally a life-or-death decision under hot, dry conditions. No simple or absolute answer can be given except one: Don't travel during a hot day. If you expect help to arrive in a day, then it would be advisable to stay put. But if no one knows your destination and rescue is unlikely, travel may be essential. Travel decisions are also dictated by the quality of maps and the expectation of finding water as well as the distance to travel to assistance. For a strong, experienced hiker, a 20-mile (32-km.) trip to water during a single night is reasonable. But what if you are ill, injured, or inexperienced? How far could you walk? The final decision may be a careful balancing of the odds, a roll of the dice, guided by every bit of energy, skill, and intelligence you are capable of mustering.

If you are forced to leave a camp or automobile, how can you find water? A good topographic map can be valuable in locating water. However, some springs and streams may dry up during the summer and fall months. During a drought, dependable sources of water may disappear. As useful as a map is, it will not reveal all available water.

Vegetation can be a guide to help locate water sources not located on maps. Cottonwood, sycamore, and willow trees grow along stream banks or near springs. Often they can be sighted from a considerable distance. Salt cedar and aspen trees often grow over subsurface water and indicate a promising place to dig. Many other plants such as cattails, arrowgrass, and sedges are excellent water indicators.

Neither plants nor maps may indicate many of the natural tanks or cisterns that collect water in the American Southwest. These natural rock depressions hold water for a few days or weeks after rain. They can be found in rocky canyons or near the base of cliffs. More dependable sources of water may be wells built by early settlers for supplying livestock. Sometimes water is deep in a well, but with wire or other nearby material you may be able to improvise a method to lower a canteen or even a shirt to get the fluid.

Many kinds of animals will travel long distances to reach wells and other water sources. In many remote desert areas, the paths of animals converge on waterholes. You can follow the paths inward like spokes of a wheel to water. In many deserts birds spend the night near water or roost in the adjacent trees. The white-winged dove can be seen flying to water in the evening and flying away from water in the morning hours. The behavior of doves and other birds, even their songs, can guide you to water supplies.

Another method to increase the chance of finding water is to study the rock formations. Rock outcrops, the bottoms of canyons, and the bases of hills may reveal the geology and terrain where water may emerge. Water will always seek the lowest point by the easiest path. Even dry stream beds may have water

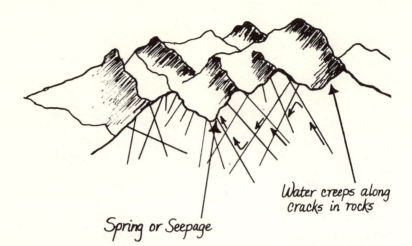

Water creeps along cracks in rocks

Spring or Seepage

Where to Look for Springs

available below the surface. Look on the outside curve of a dry stream, where water would cut into a bank. Search the lowest point of a stream bed, where the water flow has poured over rock or plunged down into the stream bed. Often animals have dug for water at these points.

Water is often at the surface or close to the surface at the base of a mountain range or at the point where a dry desert stream emerges from a rugged canyon. Look at the dip or angle of repose of geologic formations, many of which trap water in layers and carry it laterally to the base of a hill or the mouth of a canyon. Undoubtedly, over vast regions of the desert, water is impossible to find, but you can increase the likelihood of finding water with a little knowledge of geology and a little creative thinking.

In the late summer, a mountain stream may disappear into the ground or under rocks and boulders. Careful study of the geology may reveal a resistant rock layer upstream or downstream. Often a "lost" river will disappear into lava or limestone rock but suddenly emerge on the surface when the underlying base rock is exposed. A related process often takes place on seacoasts. Fresh water springs often emerge on a beach just above the low tide and provide a source of sweet water. Look for small rivulets on a sandy beach, especially when the tide is out.

In cold weather, snow or ice is difficult to melt. While it is often possible to melt snow by simply eating it, this can lead to hypothermia or chilling of the body. Carry a small piece of black plastic while traveling over snow or ice. Spread out the plastic on a sunny day. Lightly sprinkle snow on the black surface, and a considerable amount of water will melt in a short time.

Finding water at sea or in the desert brings its own problems and myths. The cruelest myth of all is a persistent belief that it is possible to drink sea water. The salt in sea water creates a serious osmotic imbalance in the body's cell walls. As a result, sea water accelerates the loss of body fluid and brings terrible suffering. To drink sea water is to invite disaster.

Another persistent myth concerns drinking human urine. Salt is usually about 2% of the total composition of urine — less than in sea water but still sufficient to accelerate dehydration. In addition to several types of salt, volatile ammonia and other organic acids are present in urine.

Popular desert myth maintains that the top of a barrel cactus can be cut open and there will be fresh, clean water in the center. Yet a barrel cactus is very tough and its thorns are a formidable obstacle. When it is opened, there is fluid inside, but it is a thick, green, slimy concoction that is difficult to get at and very bitter. Nevertheless, the pulpy material from the barrel cactus and other cactus can be useful in a solar still. However, do not expect to find cool, clear water inside this formidable cactus.

Once water is located, its purity must always be questioned. Water in swamps may be dark and acidic but not impure. Water in a north woods bog may be full of mosquito larvae but safe to drink. Conversely, clear, fresh water flowing over rocks may cause serious illness. While spring water is usually pure, there is no purification process from water merely flowing over rocks. Before backpacking was as popular as it is today, few mountain streams or springs were contaminated. However, polluted water is now fairly common in very remote areas. Amoebic dysentery, infectious hepatitis, and salmonella are diseases that can be contracted even though the fluid is cold, clear, and found in the high mountains. Therefore, even wilderness water must be purified to prevent sickness and disease.

Probably the oldest method of purifying water is to boil it for five minutes. When in the mountains, add one minute of boiling time for every 1,000 feet (300 meters) of elevation; thus at 5,000 feet (1,500 meters), water should be boiled for ten minutes instead of five minutes. It is possible to remove some of the disagreeable odors and taste from water by adding charcoal from a campfire to the water when it is boiling. To restore some of the taste, the charcoal can be filtered out and the water aerated by vigorous shaking.

Boiling will take care of most but not all of the problems of pollution. It is time consuming and also requires proper containers. Water-purification tablets, which are sold in drugstores or outdoor equipment shops, can be used to purify water by simply following the directions on the label — but many of them deteriorate with time. Kept in a pack or survival kit for some time, they may not be satisfactory. Their efficiency varies with the temperature of the water and the amount of pollution.

It is possible to purify water with household bleach: about 2 drops of bleach per quart (liter) of water if the water is clear or 4 drops if it is coudy. Let the water sit for approximately 30 minutes before drinking. Chlorine, the active disinfectant ingredient in bleach, is not effective in higher pHs such as alkaline water. (Most desert water is alkaline; it often has a soapy taste, and the edges of a water hole will have a chalky white ring.) Chlorine also breaks down into ineffective byproducts that do not disinfect water. Simple chlorination is also unpredictable with certain forms of bacteria and when water is contaminated with organic material. Hepatitis is a serious disease caused by a virus that is not destroyed by various types of chlorine treatment. You should not trust chlorination as a water purification method unless the chlorine is fresh.

Iodination is a simple, effective method of distilling or disinfecting large amounts of water. Iodine is a disinfectant that is not influenced by the temperature of the water, the pH, or other factors. The system is lightweight and fairly simple to use. Some other purification tablets are not effective in cold water, heavily polluted water, or water that has particularly resistant forms of viruses and amoebic cysts. Iodination is an efficient germicide for all viruses and amoeba.

Iodine treatment can be accomplished in three basic ways. The first is to add 8 drops of 2% tincture of iodine to a quart (liter) of water. This is very effective, but the water retains a fairly strong iodine taste which some people find objectionable. A second method is to use iodine tablets, but they lose their effectiveness with time. Approximately 20% of their effectiveness is lost with a shelf life of six months, and they lose 33% of their effectiveness when they are exposed to air for only four days.

A third and best procedure uses crystalline iodine. A one-ounce (35-milliliter) bottle with a leak-proof cap is needed. In this bottle place 4 to 8 grams of iodine crystals obtained from a drug store. The bottle should then be filled with water, capped, and shaken vigorously for 30 to 60 seconds. Hold the bottle upright for a few minutes to permit the heavy iodine crystals to fall to the bottom. The crystals themselves are not used in the disinfection process. The iodine solution becomes saturated from the crystals. Add the saturated solution, but not the crystals, to a quart of water. A one-ounce (35-milliliter) bottle of saturated iodine solution to a quart (liter) of water will purify the water in approximately 15 minutes.

A longer purification period is needed if the water is very polluted or cold. After 40 or 50 minutes, even extremely contaminated or very cold water will be purified. The crystals in the one-ounce (35-milliliter) bottle will last for almost a thousand treatments or a thousand quarts of water. The only danger is to mistakenly pour one of the crystals into the drinking water and then swallow it. However, even this should not be a serious problem if you are careful. The iodine crystal method is fast, effective, and convenient.

Loss of body water is not the only problem of dehydration. Water loss also brings a loss of salts, through both urine and sweating. Under conditions of dehydration, headaches and nausea may result from salt deficiency. Body salts are lost during the sweating process, as much as 15 grams per day prior to acclimatization. The body can tolerate a 20% – 30% loss in its salt supply with little or no problem. Craving for salt may not be an indicator of salt requirements; headaches or muscle cramps are more common symptoms.

Salt can be replaced by salt tablets or extra salting of food. Important trace salts such as magnesium are also lost during excessive sweating. Normally these salts are replaced with a balanced diet. Several commercial drinks and tablets such as ERG and Gatorade, very popular with runners, are available to backpackers and dry-country hikers.

In addition to salts, every survival kit should include materials for a survival still. This is a simple method of distilling water from soil and plant materials using the sun's energy to drive the distillation process. The important component of a solar still is a piece of clear plastic about 6 feet (2 meters) square. Black plastic, even translucent plastic, is not adequate. The plastic must be clear to be most efficient. The second item needed is a container — one that will hold approximately 2 to 4 quarts of fluid. In an emergency, however, a container may be fashioned from extra plastic film, aluminum foil, or some other waterproof material. A third component is convenient but not essential: plastic tubing, the thickness of a drinking straw, about 5 feet (1.5 meters) long. If tubing is available, water can be sucked from the container without disturbing the solar still. The components can be easily folded into a pocket-size package. For comfortable survival, one should have sufficient plastic for several stills.

The operation of a solar still is quite simple. The solar energy in sunlight passes through the plastic and is absorbed by the soil or plant material inside. Heat evaporates the moisture and it condenses on the cooler plastic above. The condensed water runs down the plastic and drops into the container where it is collected.

The illustration shows the basic side view of a solar still. Dig out a hole approximately 3 feet (1 meter) in diameter and 1½ feet deep. This can be excavated in many places, but it is important to consider the soil. Rocky areas, with gravel or sand, are the poorest places to locate the still. Such soil material does not hold much moisture. A dense loam is superior. If at all possible, locate the pit where the soil is damp and the digging easy. Once the hole is excavated, put the container inside and place the

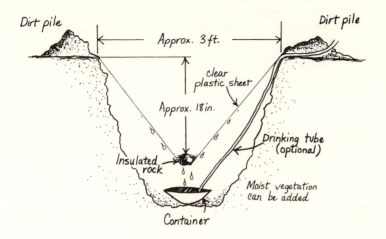

Dirt pile

Dirt pile

Approx. 3 ft.

clear plastic sheet

Approx. 18 in.

Drinking tube (optional)

Insulated rock

Moist vegetation can be added

Container

Solar Still

plastic cover over the hole. If available, place plant material, particularly chunks of barrel cactus or other pulpy cactus, into the hole. If polluted or muddy water is available, it can be poured into the hole before the cover is sealed. Hold it in place with rocks or soil around the edge. It is important to keep the edge of the plastic sealed tightly. Then push the center of the plastic down to form a cone which has an angle about 25° – 40° from the horizontal. Place a rock or some other weight directly over the container to make the conical shape. This will also reduce wind flutter. It may be essential under very warm conditions to insulate the rock weight with bark or a piece of cloth to keep it from gaining heat and melting through the plastic.

Once the process is understood, the construction of a solar still should take no more than 15 to 20 minutes. It will then take an hour or two for the air in the still to become saturated underneath the plastic film. After that, water will begin to condense on the plastic and start dripping into the container. In dry soil that has been many weeks without rain, only a small amount of water can be collected from the soil. Under these conditions, it is important to augment soil moisture by adding plant material.

But the most important rule is to use clear plastic. Some plastics, because of their surface, will tend to cause the water droplets forming on the film to drop off before they reach the container. As with other aspects of survival, experiment with various types of clear plastic to find which kind is the most wettable and which will carry a drop of water from the edge of the film down to the bottom of the cone where it will drop into the container. Also experiment by scratching the plastic with sandpaper to scarify the surface and create enough surface tension for the droplet to wind its way down to the bottom of the cone.

The production of water from a solar still will depend upon the moisture in the soil, the type of soil, and the amount of plant material in the hole. Under good conditions, the still should produce 1 to 2 quarts (liters) of water per day. After several days, the still may accumulate a crust of salt on the soil surface which will slow down the process. If soil moisture is not replaced with new plant material and subsurface moisture, move the still to avoid the salt. It is best to carry several sheets of plastic so that stills can be placed in several different sites.

Keep the still sealed because the distillation process will continue even at night, although at usually half the daytime rate. The plastic tubing will enable you to suck water out of the container, without disrupting the process of the still. Another advantage of the plastic still is the possibility of water from a summer rainstorm collecting in the bottom of the cone. It is wise to set out other containers, improvised if necessary, especially at night in case of such a rain.

Obviously you could build a larger still with a larger piece of plastic, but the size recommended for optimal use is approximately 6 feet (2 meters) square. A larger still requires a larger hole, and it is much easier to dig several small holes.

Water, that simple fluid, constantly recycled by the sun, is an essential element of wilderness survival. The cycle of early man's life was built around water and the eternal seasons. Water, a product to defend and conserve, was clearly central to life. When the mouth dries and the canteen is empty, the sun will still burn into the brain the importance of water. As common as water appears from the bathroom faucet, it remains, as always, priceless.

6

Food

Accidents and poor planning exposed several 19th-century expeditions to months, even years, of malnutrition, hunger, and starvation. The Greeley Arctic Expedition of 1881 – 84 provides one of the most ghastly records of survival.

Adolphus William Greeley and his men were forced to spend an extra winter in the North. The men became weak, irritable, and obsessed with talk of food. Trust among members of the group disappeared as food was stolen during the long Arctic nights. By January 1884, members of the group died and the survivors became bitter. The strong robbed the weak; one man was shot for stealing food. They fought over thongs and skins as sources of food and consumed their boots, even their pants.

When rescued in June, only seven of the party were found. All pain of hunger had ceased; the men were reduced to skeletons with swollen joints and feet. Their abdominal cavities were shrunken and almost in contact with the vertebral column. The graves of eighteen others were found nearby.

The history of humankind has been, in part, an epic search for food. The fear of hunger has always directed human actions and attitudes. It was probably the fear of hunger that shifted nomadic hunting and gathering skills to herding animals and growing crops. Somewhere between 6000 and 5000 B.C., planting and reaping crops began.

With domestic agriculture came the rise of cities and what we call civilization. However, the earliest written records of cities tell of periodic starvation and hunger. Descriptions of human hunger, in time of war or drought, are grim. But an understanding of the symptoms of hunger and malnutrition is helpful in dealing with this ancient dread when planning for survival in the wilderness.

Normally, a person balances food intake with energy expenditure. Regulated by the central nervous system, we normally eat a sufficient amount of food to maintain body weight, to meet energy and basal metabolic requirements. But stress, in a variety of forms, can upset this balanced process. Exceptional physical activity or drastic environmental change disturbs the normal process. The appetite is also changed by nonphysical factors such as psychological stress. Various drugs, infections, or disease may drastically alter food preferences. Individual appetite and food requirements are influenced by genetic factors, physical condition, and adaptability to stress. Therefore, a discussion of food and food requirements must always be tempered by a consideration of individuality and environmental differences.

It has become a truism of survival literature that food is the least important of all the body needs. True, a healthy person can live three weeks or more without food, provided he is inactive. However, the physiological and psychological problems of starvation are numerous. While personal food requirements are variable, the ability to work and travel is largely restricted by a limited diet.

During the first few days without food, the body consumes its surplus fat. It then begins to respond rather quickly to the lack of food. The basal metabolic rate, the rate at which food and energy are burned in the body, slows. Skin temperature begins to drop. After several days without food, the core temperature is also reduced and the heart rate slows. This automatic response of the body will prolong life in a favorable environment, because the existing energy stores of fat in the body are stretched.

However, if one is out in very cold temperatures, the drop in core temperature may well be fatal because of hypothermia. During the later stages of starvation, the body begins to break down protein and muscle. Weakness, dull reactions, and other physical problems degrade the body and spirit. Interestingly, sensory mechanisms such as sight, hearing, and smell remain robust. Some experimental data suggest that hearing is actually improved, evidence that supports an adage that "hunger sharpens the senses."

Fasting has been long recognized as a means to heighten the senses. Self-denial is common with many of the world's religions and can be a healthy, invigorating practice. Conversely, other individuals and cultures enjoy feasts and overeating. The human body has evolved with the ability to adapt to various amounts of food. Food consumption and taste are related to a person's family type and cultural background.

The body is also capable of a wide variation in daily diet. Diets throughout the world vary tremendously in content from nearly all-meat diets to nearly all-vegetable diets, with numerous combinations in between. The human body can adapt to a radical change in diet rapidly with very few signs of discomfort. There is little reason why a healthy, hungry person cannot accept a new and different diet. In an anthropological sense, this ability to adjust to a wide variety of foods is a reason why primitive man colonized most of the world's land surface, in contrast to other animals, whose habitat was limited by a selective diet.

Food biases developed in modern society are not related to the nutritional value of food. Most preferences for food are culturally determined. These cultural food preferences must be overcome in a survival situation to get an adequate intake of food. Two examples of food bias involve the fox and dog. In the Western world, both of these animals are not considered edible, yet the fox is regarded as a delicacy in parts of Russia and the dog was a favorite meal in China. Many of the western American Indians considered dog as food for special occasions. The Paiute Indians of the Great Basin regarded crickets as a delicacy. Ants and other insects were considered not only nutritious but a special treat.

During an emergency, it is difficult to make a transition

immediately from a modern diet to wild foods. But it helps to begin learning more about the environment that produces various edible animals and plants. It is also imperative to know how to prepare foods so that cultural biases can be masked or mastered. If cultural tastes are not conquered, desperation may result.

The Donner Party, a group of farmers bound for California in 1846, provided one of the grimmest survival sagas and an unfortunate lesson on the inability to adapt. The party of eighty-one people was overtaken by deep snows in the Sierra Nevada. Unorganized and without discipline, they allayed their fears with unrealistic hopes. After weeks of hunger, they were driven to eat hides, bark, and pine twigs. They pounced on mice like cats. Finally, as the group began to die one by one, they resorted to cannibalism. Before the remnants were rescued, forty-five had died.

Today's backpacker is unlikely to face such an ordeal. In summer, knowing a few edible plants, as well as poisonous ones, can make a difference in survival. Herbs or wild onions can be gathered and incorporated into freeze-dried meals carried in one's pack. A boater can practice new fishing techniques and a skier can decipher animal tracks and learn simple methods of trapping. As with most aspects of survival, a knowledge of plants, animals, and the environment is essential to a comfortable, secure, enjoyable outdoor experience.

In addition to understanding a wilderness environment, you should understand basic concepts of food chemistry. To maintain good mental and physical condition, it is important to eat nutritional foods. When you are physically active, the process of starvation, along with the physical and mental deterioration, is accelerated. There are two basic food components. The quantity constituents are fats, carbohydrates, and proteins. The minor constituents, minerals and vitamins, are important even in very small quantities. Most foods contain a mixture of these components, and a balance will be achieved in a normal diet.

Fats, the first of the major constituents, are used to generate the heat of the body and to supply energy. Fat is an important source of energy because it yields twice as much energy by weight as carbohydrate or protein. Solid fats are found in meats in the form of lard, drippings, and suet. Milk fat is contained in various dairy products. During extremely cold conditions, fat is required to generate heat. Arctic veteran Vilhjalmur Stefansson regarded fat as the most important food in the North.

Fatty foods also provide important vitamins such as A, D, E, and K, as well as essential fatty acids. Individual dietary requirements vary greatly, but cold and high altitude tend to reduce the body's store of fat. Usually, people in cold environments crave more fatty foods. At high elevations, however, probably because of the lack of oxygen, fat becomes difficult for the body to utilize, so mountaineers usually consume higher levels of carbohydrate.

Carbohydrates, the second major food constituent, are used by the body for quick energy and in muscle movement. They can also be converted by the body to fat. Carbohydrates supply approximately two-thirds of the immediate energy produced by the body. They are found in seeds, leaves, root vegetables and tubers, fruits, nuts, animal blood, and some internal organs. Some refined foods such as sugar and starch are almost pure carbohydrate, and their use in the form of candy prior to and during strenuous hiking or climbing is a common technique to improve physical performance.

Sources of carbohydrates also supply many of the minerals that are needed for the regulation of normal body metabolism. Sodium, potassium, calcium, and iron are some of the most important minerals. Sodium and potassium are often depleted by excessive sweating and water loss. Extra iron is sometimes needed at high elevations. Many of the water-soluble B group of vitamins, as well as vitamin C, are found in carbohydrates. The B and C vitamins are especially prone to depletion during times of stress. For this reason, many individuals carry supplements on extended trips.

Proteins are the third and final type of major foods the body requires. The most common source of protein is the lean meat of animals. It is also found in milk, cheese, eggs, seeds, and legumes such as beans and peas.

The three major food constituents are usually the chief concern when eating. But the minor components, such as vitamins, are essential. ("Vitamin" means essential to life.) Tiny amounts of these compounds are necessary for the regulation of various processes in the human physiology. They serve as catalysts for certain metabolic reactions and are the source of many chemicals the body manufactures. Vitamins are found in varying amounts in plants and animals. An extreme vitamin deficiency can cause a disease such as scurvy; lesser deficiencies can result in bruising, skin sores, and bleeding gums. There are people who believe that some lack of vitamin C results in more colds and flu. The complex of B vitamins, such as B-1, 2, 6, and 12, increases the body's ability to resist cold and frostbite.

An excess of vitamins can also be a problem. The Eskimos and early Arctic travelers initially believed polar bear liver was poisonous. Encountering this common belief, Vilhjalmur Stefansson experimented by eating several polar bear livers to determine if the liver was indeed poisonous. Sometimes he developed headaches and nausea. Later research discovered it was the excess of vitamin A in the liver that caused illness. If the heart, kidney, and other organs of a bear are consumed, some people will become ill within two to four hours after eating. There are various symptoms — drowsiness, sluggishness, irritability, and severe headaches. During laboratory experiments, some individuals were found to have peeling skin and painful sores around their face. Rarely would a person eating polar bear livers or other animal organs be subject to vitamin poisoning. However, those who carry vitamin supplements on backcountry trips should be aware of the problem. There is always a temptation to eat them if food is scarce. It is possible to overload the body, especially with fat-soluble vitamins such as A.

Minerals are another type of minor foods needed by the body. They are often depleted from the body during very dry conditions. A high loss of water, especially by sweating, carries with it various types of minerals like salt flushed out of the body. The shortage of salts can cause muscle cramps and aches, headaches, and a general sense of discomfort. Salt tablets to correct this problem should be part of any survival ration in desert conditions. Many starving people have a craving for salt. Consumption of water is high and salt intake, if available, is several times the normal level. One result, edema, or the excessive accumulation of body fluid, usually is noticeable first as a puffy face or swollen ankles.

An excess of salt causes problems when traveling at sea. Salt, without an adequate source of water, causes thirst, dehydration, stomach ulcerations, and eventually salt poisoning — the body's inability to rid itself of excessive amounts of salt either through urine or perspiration because of a lack of water.

With a knowledge of the basic foods the body requires, the next step is to understand the various sources of food available in the wild. The most obvious sources are large mammals — such as elk, deer, or moose — but they are difficult to capture by an inexperienced person without a firearm. Much easier to capture are many small nutritious creatures that can serve as adequate food if a person can overcome cultural biases. The porcupine, slow and stupid, has long been considered a good source of food. Squirrels, especially many ground squirrels, and rabbits are fairly easy to capture. Even mice, voles, and small rodents can be consumed. Additionally, capturing these small animals and other creatures requires little in equipment.

Fishing is a culturally acceptable method of securing food. It is prudent either to carry fishhooks and line in an emergency survival kit or to be able to improvise these materials in the wild. Fishhooks can be made out of aluminum can tabs, a piece of wire, a piece of shell, or even two small twigs tied together. A good exercise is to try to determine what would serve as a fishhook. It might be safety pins, or wire, or a small piece of wood. Try to carve a fishhook out of a bone, a thorn, or a piece of seashell. Even a small GI can opener can be used as a lure.

It is also possible to probe gently under the banks of small tributary streams for fish that lurk in the shadows of the roots of trees. Fish can be caught by hand, but this method takes time and a great deal of patience and skill. Another method is to drive fish, even small minnows found in shallow water, into traps woven of willow or other material. A rock or log barrier can be used to make a narrow gap where the trap is placed; then the fish are driven into the trap. It is also possible to attract fish at night with a light, a torch, or a flashlight. Although all these methods can be used in an emergency, it is more efficient to carry some line and small hooks in a survival kit. Use willow or other flexible branches and make several fishing sets from the line, then bait the hooks. It is often productive to fish at night and to

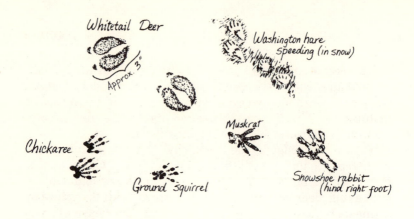

Whitetail Deer

Approx. 3"

Washington hare speeding (in snow)

Chickaree

Muskrat

Ground squirrel

Snowshoe rabbit (hind right foot)

Some Common Animal Tracks

leave set lines fastened to branches or to some floating object overnight. Placing several baited lines overnight while resting or sleeping is an efficient use of time. Fish can also be caught through ice, by netting, by shooting, even by poisoning. But the most dependable way is through the use of a few hooks and some line.

During an emergency, small animals are relatively easy to capture with patience and a creative approach. Just as a city has ethnic neighborhoods, concentrations of business and industry, the wildlands have specialized animal habitats. It helps to know the life history of an animal, where it lives, where it wanders, and its tracks. This is the key to placing snares at the mouth of a burrow or on an animal path. Many small mammals daily travel to water along paths where they may stumble into a trap.

Once an animal's burrows and trails are understood, trapping is much easier. Several types of traps can be used with various degrees of success in the wilderness. Traps normally used against larger animals crush the prey and require considerable effort in their construction. A very large rock or a log is set up and designed to fall on the animal and kill or disable it. The easiest traps to set up have a simple loop attached to a weight or a branch. Other traps may be a pit, box, or some other cage to hold the animal in place until the hunter arrives.

Each of these traps has advantages and disadvantages, but

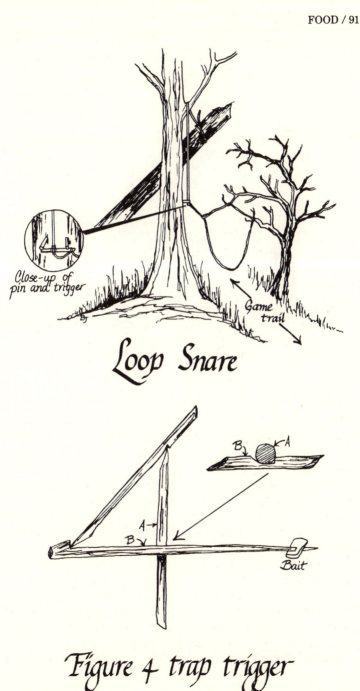

Close-up of
pin and trigger

Game
trail

Loop Snare

B A

A
B

Bait

Figure 4 trap trigger

Small Game Snare

the snare trap is the easiest to use. The snare has simple components, a loop, designed to catch the head of an animal. A loop, made from shoelaces, a strip of cloth, a nylon cord, or a length of strong wire, is anchored to a rock, bush, or tree to strangle an animal when it attempts to get away. More elaborate versions of a snare have trigger and spring devices. A survival kit should include fishing line, other nylon cord, or fine wire to improvise snares. Many other types of traps can be made. The figure-four trigger is easy to construct and is a common method of setting a deadfall or box trap. Box traps can be created by weaving willows or other sticks together and balancing heavy logs or rocks with a figure-four trigger. When tripped, the animal is crushed or disabled. Cord can be made from the inner bark of some trees or from shrub or plant fiber twisted together. These can also be used to make tools, to weave traps, or to construct snares. Animals may be smoked or flooded out of their dens into waiting snares or box traps.

A survivalist can also build tools for hunting equipment, such as bows and arrows, slingshots, boomerangs, bolas, and other devices to capture animals. But the simplest and most effective tool, one commonly used by many primitive people, is a throwing stick. A stout piece of wood perhaps 18 inches to 2 feet (45 – 60 cm.) long is thrown at rabbits, squirrels, or other animals. As it twists through the air it is apt to hit the animal, stun it or break a leg, and make capture easier. It is often possible to approach an animal indirectly in the wild by tracking in zig-zag fashion closer and closer to it. Many animals, such as a rabbit, may stay in a hiding position until a person is quite close. By using this slow, indirect approach, you can stun or kill the animal with a throwing stick or even a rock.

Using a rodent skewer, you can successfully capture small game hiding in burrows. The skewer is merely a willow stick or other flexible branch, up to 6 feet (2 meters) in length, with a branched fork or prong in the end. Watch for a ground squirrel, a rabbit, or another burrowing animal. If the rodent runs down a hole, poke the flexible stick down the hole into the nooks and side burrows to determine if it may be reached. If the animal is felt, quickly jab and twist the stick into the fur to catch and hold the animal. Gently pull it to the surface by keeping the tension on the twisted stick in its fur. Once it emerges, dispatch it and add it to the stew pot.

Many techniques of hunting animals may be useful in a survival situation. However, there is an important legal consideration. Hunting is not allowed at all times of the year or in national parks. Humans are deadly and efficient predators, and virtually all birds and mammals are protected by state fish and game laws. If it is essential to practice capturing animals, this must be done during the legal hunting season.

In learning to capture wildlife, it helps to know some basic principles of ecology. The so-called edge effect is important. Many animals live on the edge of dense woods, meadows, marshes, or other environments. Often an animal seeks shelter in heavy woods but feeds in an open meadow. Other animals reside in dry country yet travel to marshes or streams to drink and to find food. Their pathways between these two environments are usually obvious. Animal tracks and droppings are distinctive, so are feeding activities. These signs represent valuable information that can be used in successful hunting.

Riparian habitats are especially productive. Biologically, the areas near water have great diversity and produce many creatures. Snakes and reptiles are associated with streambanks and lakeshores and can be good sources of protein. Rattlesnake is a well-known delicacy to many outdoorsmen. Fried or roasted, the meat is often compared to chicken. Many snakes are easy to capture with a forked stick or by smashing their head with a rock. Care must always be used. It is important with rattlesnakes to cut off and bury the head so that it cannot be stepped on. Even after the head of a rattlesnake has been cut off, its fangs can remain poisonous.

Termites and caterpillars are high in protein and fat. The larvae of many insects also are high in fat and contain essential minerals. Locusts and grasshoppers can be fried to provide excellent sources of protein and vitamins. Earthworms are another source of protein.

Birds and bird eggs, which are especially nutritious and high in protein, are another source of accessible food, at least during some months of the year. A knowledge of birds is helpful, including where their eggs may be found and how they may be captured. Understanding their habitat will lead to nests and young birds during spring and summer. Often it is difficult to overcome our cultural bias. For the avid bird watcher, the thought of robbing a songbird's nest for its eggs may be repulsive. Yet properly prepared, the eggs and the very young birds are nutritious and may be essential to survival.

The best way to prepare foods in an acceptable manner is to make a stew. Place in the stew, not just larvae and insects, but rodents and other small animals that have been caught and mashed. The entire concoction can be simmered. A stew is much more palatable than an earthworm. Survival stews must mask the appearance of the exotic ingredients.

Most mammals and birds need preparation for comfortable eating. Small animals and birds are easy to skin. Carefully slit the skin on the underside with a knife or a freshly broken, sharp rock. Once a slit is made, the skin can be pulled off. Do not waste fur or feathers; they may be used as fish lures, for warmth, or for many other purposes.

Skin around to backbone, one side at a time

Prop open body cavity

Remove + use:
Brain
Heart
Lungs
Liver
Kidneys

Skinning out a Large Animal

After the animal is skinned, slit open the abdominal cavity and clean out the intestines and organs. Save the heart, lungs, liver, kidneys, and stomach, which are edible. Be careful not to contaminate the meat with material from the intestine, bladder, or sex organs. Gutting and skinning an animal allows it to cool quickly and reduces the likelihood of spoiling.

In larger animals, the eyes, tongue, and brain should be saved. Blood from animals can be used to make sausage and is a useful and nutritious salt substitute, but don't try to use blood as a substitute for water. Large animals should be cut into smaller pieces to make handling easier. Wrap the meat in leaves or grass and store in a cool place away from insects and other animals. In cold weather, cut the meat into small pieces before it freezes solid.

Although cooking of most foods, including meat, is not entirely necessary, there are advantages. In a survival situation cooking can help overcome the psychological barrier of eating unusual foods. It helps to make foods more appealing, more palatable, and, in some cases, safer to eat. There are several ways of cooking, which depend upon the situation and the availability of utensils. Boiling is an efficient method because the broth can be used for the maximum nutrients. A container in which to boil food can be built out of birch bark, a discarded can, or a woven basket sealed with pine pitch. It is heated by dropping hot rocks from a campfire into the water until boiling occurs. The method is time consuming but effective under primitive conditions. Roasting is a fine method of cooking meat. A skewer can be made and meat roasted over coals. Coating the meat with mud, then placing it on hot coals, saves the juices and minimizes heat loss to burning. Hot coals are superior for roasting meat to flames which tend to charcoal the meat instead of cooking it.

Baking is another method that is used throughout the world. You can wrap game in grass or leaves and bury it in the earth below a fire. Baking game by coating a fish or bird or mammal in mud approximately ½ inch (1.5 cm.) thick is a slow but tasty method. Build an oven in the ground by digging a pit 2 or 3 feet (up to 1 meter) deep and lining it with rocks. Start a large fire in the pit and wait for it to burn down. Rake out the largest hot coals, then place the meat or animal in the fire pit. Cover the entire pit with dirt, hot ashes, and hot rocks. Depending on its size, the meat should be ready in eight to twelve hours. It can be left in the ground for a full day and still be hot and juicy when uncovered. Pit baking is a good method of preparing food when you leave camp to go out foraging for other materials. You can return confident of having a warm, tasty meal.

Frying, probably the least desirable method of preparing food, destroys many useful minerals and nutrients.

Thousands of plants can be used as food. You need only some knowledge and understanding of plants to have many nutritious vegetables close at hand. A simple tool will help in gathering edible plants. Find a stick, about 1 inch (3 cm.) thick and up to 3 feet (1 meter) long. Rub the head of the stick on a coarse rock until it is reasonably sharp and harden the point in a fire. Such a stick is useful for digging out the tubers of certain plants.

Of the many tens of thousands of plants in the world, only a few are dangerous to eat. Many excellent guides to edible plants are available. Consult an appropriate guidebook for your region and begin a study of the plants. Understanding even a few

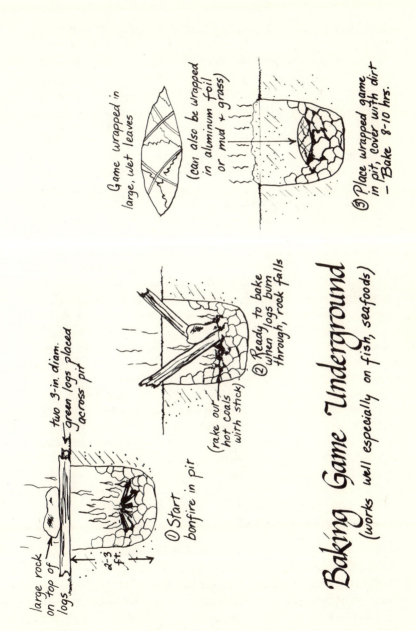

Game wrapped in large, wet leaves

(can also be wrapped in aluminum foil or mud + grass)

③ Place wrapped game in pit, cover with dirt — Bake 8-10 hrs.

large rock on top of logs

two 3-in. diam. green logs placed across pit

2-3 ft.

① Start bonfire in pit

(rake out hot coals with stick)

② Ready to bake when logs burn through, rock falls

Baking Game Underground
(works well especially on fish, seafoods)

dependable and widely dispersed edible plants will greatly enhance your survival confidence. In an emergency you may have to try some plants that are unknown. Be cautious, because the symptoms of a few poisonous plants may not emerge for twelve hours or more. However, in an emergency the following procedure can be followed.

To test a plant to determine whether or not it is edible, place a small portion in your mouth, making sure not to swallow it. Then wait for any burning, stinging, or numbing sensation. If there is none, chew and eat a small portion of the plant. Wait several hours to see if there are any adverse symptoms, such as a burning sensation, numbness in the mouth, or an upset stomach. After several hours, cook a small amount. Many edible plants must be boiled in water, sometimes two or more times with the boiled water poured off, to cleanse the material of strong chemicals. The water must be poured off and not drunk. If someone should be poisoned by a plant, it is important to induce vomiting by the use of Ipecac in a first-aid kit or by a finger probing the throat. Keep the victim both warm and quiet.

Some poisonous plants deserve on-sight recognition. Probably the most important one is water hemlock, a species of hemlock used to brew the tea given Socrates. A piece of hemlock the size of a peanut will be fatal to most people. Hemlock, one of the most poisonous plants in North America, grows in a wide variety of environments and areas. Poisonous plants are a complex subject and detailed information should be sought by a serious herbalist. Some garlic and wild onion plants will merely taint milk and dairy products. If carelessly handled, other plants, notably the cactus family, may cause mechanical injury. Still other plants, such as some mustards and flax, produce poisonous seeds. Prussic acid, or hydrocyanic acid, is produced by some flax, chokecherry, and laurel species. With many poisonous plants, the toxicity varies from season to season and according to location. Finally, many plants are poisonous upon contact. Reactions to these plants vary with the susceptibility of individuals. The most common plant causing a reaction upon contact, or dermatitis, is poison ivy. Poison oak and sumac are also irritating plants, as are various species of nettles. Some mushrooms, such as the toadstool, and common garden plants such as

Water Hemlock

Poison Hemlock

LE

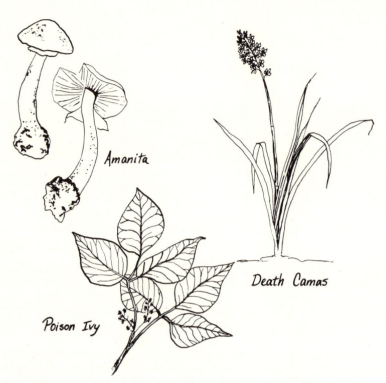

Amanita

Death Camas

Poison Ivy

iris, poinsettia, hyacinth, daffodil, and lily-of-the-valley are also poisonous.

Sometimes several parts of a plant can be eaten. Seeds are a good source of protein. Although gathering the small seeds of many grasses and herbs is time consuming, they are well worth the trouble it takes to gather them. They can be beaten off the plants into baskets or onto a woven mat. Dry husks and dirt can be winnowed by blowing on the seeds or tossing them into the air. Certain grasses hold their seed and provide a source of protein during the cold periods of the year when other plant foods have withered. Overall, the various species of rice, wheat, corn, oats, and other grasses provide the largest single source of food in the world. Seeds can be ground into flour, added to stews, or roasted. Some backpackers carry a small seed sprouter in their pack and have fresh sprouts at their camp. The seeds of many plants can be dried and stored for future use.

Among the largest classes of edible plant foods are wild fruits. Blackberries, blueberries, plums, and grapes often grow abundantly in the wild and make a fine addition to any meal. Yucca

Common Arrowhead

Cattail

Dandelion

Prickly Pear Cactus

Mariposa Lily

Wild Onion

fruits were often roasted by early Americans and described as equal to apple pie. A common riparian tree is the papaw, whose fruit supplied the hungry men of the Lewis and Clark expedition as they approached St. Louis in 1806. In the western territory, the members often enjoyed serviceberry and added it to their pemmican, a mixture of dried meat, fruit, and animal fat.

Various pine nuts were an important part of American Indian diets. Nuts can be roasted, ground into flour, even ground and mixed with water to form a nutritious drink. Oak acorns, chestnuts, and hazelnuts are also edible and nutritious.

Some water plants are edible. Among the best known is the cattail, whose pollen is a rich source of protein. The young shoots in early spring taste somewhat like celery. In the winter, the root stalks can be gathered, even under ice, to provide a useful source of carbohydrate. The inner bark of poplars, cottonwood, aspen, birch, and willows can be eaten in an emergency. The inner bark of pine, palatable especially in the spring, is a source of vitamin C. Plant material can be used to construct mats and baskets, and in other crafts. Plants can be used as dyes or merely to decorate a campsite and lift the spirit.

While the botany of edible plants is sometimes complex, there are many other benefits from learning about them. Rosehips are a very good source of vitamins A and C. Wild onion leaves may provide a good insect repellant. The inner bark of chokecherry can be used as a tea to stop diarrhea. The roots of burdock can be made into a salve for burns and wounds, and an infusion of comfrey leaves is also effective. There are literally hundreds of medicinal plants and thousands of edible plants in the United States and Canada.

Knowledge of a few edible plants or of how to prepare a tea in the wilds adds a new dimension to any outdoor excursion. Euell Gibbons, the famous herbalist and botanist, who wrote several useful books on this subject, related his delight in finding several edible plants on the White House lawns. Similar delight and pleasure can be experienced along a trail or on any outdoor trip.

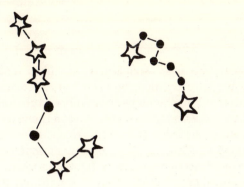

7

Travel and Routefinding

Many years ago Enos Mills, the father of Rocky Mountain National Park, became snowblind high in the Rockies. Mills remained calm and, using nature's signs, began to work his way slowly out of the mountains. Even before he started, Mills had a clear mental map of the route — he had remembered important details of the previous day's climb. Although unable to use his eyes, he found blaze marks on trees with his fingers. He checked his direction from trees that grew only on north slopes and lichens that grew on the north sides of rocks. To determine the topography nearby, he shouted and listened to the pattern of echoes. Finally, he smelled aspen smoke, a common fuel for cook stoves. He followed the scent for 2 miles farther to safety. Stranded high in the mountains, Mills had no choice but to find his way down to safety. However, the first decision in routefinding is whether to travel or to wait for assistance.

Once you decide to travel, you may find it difficult to reverse. Although you must decide carefully, you may have to do so quickly. To reach the best conclusion, you must consider many variables in a complex matrix.

Physical condition is the first variable to consider. Your evaluation of physical condition must be based on experience and realistic expectations. You should be relatively certain how far you can travel in the mountains, in a desert, or in the water. Modify your expectations by considering injuries, illness, or other debilitating factors. Although you are an experienced hiker, you may be recovering from an illness. Injuries may limit your strength, endurance, or skill. Obviously, in a group, the most capable persons are selected to seek help or to lead the routefinding.

Often, critical injuries result in hasty decisions. Some may rush off to find help unprepared. First, a person requiring medical help must be treated and made as comfortable as possible. At times, it may be better to slowly assist someone out of the mountains, instead of leaving him alone and unable to take care of himself. Hypothermia, heat stroke, or severe bleeding must be treated in the field prior to seeking aid. At other times, a person alone and injured has no other choice but to deal with his own injuries and try to get out somehow, no matter how difficult it may appear.

A consideration of food and water must always be part of the decision matrix. Survivors of a plane crash in the mountains may have shelter, firewood, and water close at hand, yet during cold weather, travel downhill will bring warmer temperatures, less snow, and possible assistance. After a crash in the desert, however, travel downhill would bring hot temperatures, less shade, and decreasing chances of finding water. The supply of emergency rations and water must be incorporated into a decision to stay or to travel. A stranded auto, an old cabin, a damaged plane may have equipment or useful survival gear that can't be carried. In such cases, it might be best to stay and wait for rescue. Yet at other times, shelter or rescue may be only a short distance away and the decision to travel is obvious.

Location is critical. Is it known or not? How far is assistance? Is the terrain easy to traverse or dangerous? Sometimes a decision involves the choice of going over a known route or going over an unknown route for an unknown distance. Timing and weather must be considered. A party stranded in a mountain storm may need to wait for clear weather to assure a safe trip. In other circumstances, inadequate food or shelter may necessitate travel during a dangerous storm. A wait of two or three days may well prove fatal. But a desert traveler will always want to wait until cooler hours to travel. Even the phase of the moon will guide travelers and influence decisions.

In desert regions, your objective is often a critical question. Is the route toward a single point like a cabin or a spring that may be hard to find? Or is your objective a highway or mountain range that is difficult to miss? If the target is a cabin or a river, it may be important to aim for one side of it. In other words, be certain to head upstream from a cabin, then once the stream is reached the choice is clear — head downstream to reach the cabin. If you hike toward a single point and don't find it, you may be confused about which way to turn, left or right. Therefore, it is better to aim at one side or the other and be certain of the final destination to avoid backtracking.

The likelihood of rescue is another important consideration. Will a search party know where to look? Does someone know the group's route and destination or was it changed at the last minute? What is the likelihood of prompt, efficient rescue? Climbers in national parks such as Yosemite and Grand Teton expect skilled rescuers. Yet remote mountain ranges may not have any organization available to assist an injured party.

Often the best decision is to remain at the site of an accident and wait for rescue. Other times that decision may be fatal. A young woman lost in the northern Rockies patiently awaited rescue and recorded her experiences in a journal. Over a year later her skeleton was found and the journal revealed her unrealistic hope for rescue. No one even knew where she had gone hiking. No rescue was ever organized to search for her.

A plane carrying a Uruguayan soccer team crashed in the Andes several years ago. The vivid account of their survival struggle is told in the book *Alive*. High in the rugged Andes, unsure of their location, the survivors elected to stay with the plane. Later, after searchers had given up, the group eventually turned to cannibalism. Finally, two men decided to hike out of the mountains and find help; yet they delayed the decision until their food was nearly exhausted and their physical condition severely impaired. Fortunately they were successful, and several of the group were found and rescued.

After considering all variables and reaching a decision to

walk out, be sure to walk properly. Walking is simple and most people have been doing it since they were a year old. Still, to walk cross country efficiently and easily is a skill that many may not appreciate. Physical condition is important, but even those in poor condition can use their weight and body conservatively. The most common mistake made by walkers is to travel too fast. Go slowly, deliberately, with steady and regular breathing. Pace is the key to a comfortable walk. If you are in doubt as to the proper pace, slow down and eventually it will develop. Don't force the pace. In a group, the pace should be based on the slowest in the party, not the fastest.

While walking, travel ahead with your eyes. Look for the best and easiest route, while detouring around barriers in the path. If possible, don't climb over rocks and logs. A young woman hiking out of Grand Canyon on a summer day began by stepping on top of each rock barrier that frequently blocked the trail. She soon learned that lifting her weight and pack in this manner would add up to many tons of work, most of it unnecessary. Avoid barriers where possible and plan a route at the same contour to avoid gaining or losing elevation.

Breathe rhythmically. If walking or climbing results in panting or gasping for breath, the rate of travel is much too fast. Rest periodically, about five or ten minutes out of every hour. Don't rest so long that your muscles are cool and stiff when you start again. Take excellent care of your feet. Stop to change socks if possible, and cool the feet to prevent blisters. Never travel or plan a backpacking trip without adhesive bandages, moleskin, or other first-aid material for the feet. Make sure to break in your boots before you leave home.

When traveling uphill, switch back and forth up the slope whenever possible. Angle up a hill so you can hike slowly but steadily. Don't fight a slope or struggle straight uphill but relax and patiently overcome the barrier. When going up a slope, place each foot carefully on the ground. Make sure footing is safe and secure. Smoothly transfer the weight from one leg to the other. On a steep slope, pause for a fraction of a second before the next step, but make the entire pace smooth. Don't try to climb on your toes; place the foot flat on the ground.

If the slope becomes too steep, use your hands for balance.

Keep your body center out from the slope whenever possible. A good rule is to keep your body an arm's length from the hillside and, as climbers say, "Don't hug the rock." Don't lean into a hill, even though that is the natural tendency, as footing is more likely to fail when leaning in than leaning out. If you should fall it will always be into a hillside. For this reason, always carry an axe or other heavy object on the downslope or downhill side. That way, when you fall you are less likely to strike an axe or other object. If possible, keep the other hand free for balance.

Test all hand and footholds on a hillside before transferring body weight. Use the three-point system. Distribute your body weight on at least three points while crossing a steep slope. In other words, move only one limb at a time. Have two good handholds and one good foothold when moving the fourth point, the foot. Or have both feet firmly planted and one handhold before moving the other hand. That way you can safely move on steep and hazardous slopes.

Climbing down steep hills is far more strenuous than it first appears to be. Muscles and tendons tire from holding the combined weight of both body and pack as you accelerate two or three feet with each step downhill. Your knees and legs tire from catching most of this weight after thousands of steps. Sprained ankles, knees, and blisters are more apt to result from downhill rather than uphill travel. When traveling downhill, keep your knees bent slightly with each step to cushion the strain on your legs. Most important, don't get going too fast, but stay in control; otherwise you may twist an ankle and fall. On steep slopes where handholds are needed, try climbing down facing sideways.

When climbing steep slopes or hills use a balanced, rhythmical pace. If you dislodge a rock and others are below, warn them immediately. Mountain courtesy demands that the highest hiker or climber be especially careful not to dislocate rocks. Loose rocks are impossible to avoid, so stay to one side or another of the person above you whenever possible. When climbing a steep gully or slope that funnels the rock down, keep on the lookout for barrriers that you can hide behind. A large rock or logs will deflect a bounding rock and help you to avoid injury. If the person above you enters an area with much talus or loose rock, seek shelter until the area is passed. In some cases the person above may have no choice but to warn the one below to seek shelter and then clean the route of loose rocks.

Inexperienced hikers and campers often rely on others for leadership and navigation, but often the person who appears to be experienced may make mistakes or be too preoccupied with other matters or just forget to bring a compass and other pieces of critical equipment. Everyone should learn routefinding and share in the experience. Begin by noting the surrounding terrain, learn the use of a map and compass, and take an active role in routefinding and navigation. A good way to begin learning orienteering is to take a college or university course. Orienteering develops skills with maps and a compass, and teaches how to travel cross country with confidence.

Map reading is an essential wilderness skill. However, most maps — Forest Service, National Park, and highway, for example — illustrate only the main peaks, roads, lakes, and other major details. Such maps, often called planimetric, do not have sufficient detail for wilderness travel. Other government agencies such as the Geological Survey are responsible for surveying and printing topographic maps. Such maps can be ordered directly from the Geological Survey or purchased in map stores, as well as in parks, hiking, and other equipment stores. Some bookstores and engineering supply houses also stock maps for their particular area.

Topographic maps and a complete understanding of how to interpret them are essential for comfortable, intelligent wilderness travel. A modern topographic map is an exciting description of the earth and its features. It is a fascinating story told by its own unique symbols and spins a tale that brings different messages to the geologist, the geographer, the hiker, and the biologist. Basically, a topographic map is a line-and-symbol representation of natural and certain man-made features on the surface of the land. What distinguishes a topographic map from a planimetric map is the use of contour lines to illustrate the shape of the land. Such a map shows the location and shape of mountains, valleys, and plains, as well as the networks of streams and rivers.

The interpretation of map symbols is essential to understanding the language of maps. Many of the common symbols are printed on some maps. The Geological Survey provides a guidebook to the symbols, as do many books on routefinding and orienteering. Colors such as blue for water, green for forests, brown for grasslands or desert, illustrate some of the features. Man-made objects like power lines, roads, and buildings are illustrated by black lines and symbols. The map reader needs practice and imagination to visualize hills, valleys, cliffs, and other features. Before going into a wilderness area, study a topo map with an experienced friend. Visualize and discuss the terrain, the route anticipated, as well as streams, lakes, rock cliffs, and other dominant features. Compare them later to the wilderness reality that you encounter. Check a map frequently on a trip. Pinpoint stream crossings, trail junctions, and other items. Develop your proficiency until you can quickly compare map points to reality.

Purchase a good compass. Learn how it works and how to orient yourself with a map and compass. Learn the declination for your area from a topographic map. Declination, the difference between true north and magnetic north, varies from one area to another. In the far north, declination can change from year to year. A compass points to magnetic north or the

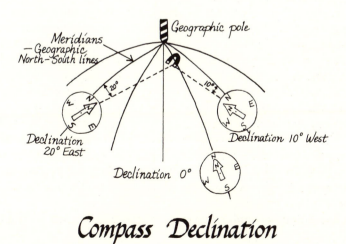

Compass Declination

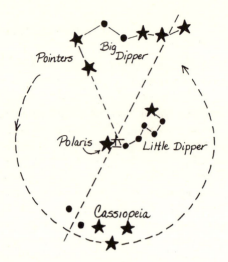

Direction from the Stars

magnetic pole. True north and north on the map will be two different points. Calibrate the compass to the declination of the area to avoid considerable errors in navigation.

At times the wilderness traveler will be without a map or compass. In this situation, there are a few general rules to assist in routefinding. First and most obvious to everyone is the fact that the sun and moon travel from east to west. Depending on the latitude, or distance from the equator, and the season of the a year, the sun will rise from the southeast to the northeast portion of the sky. Twice a year, once in the spring and once in the fall, during the equinox the sun will rise due east. It will set in the southwest portion in the winter months and in the northwest in the summer months.

Certain stars are excellent directional indicators. The Polaris, or North Star, is located very close to due north throughout the year. Other predominant constellations, such as Orion, also provide directional information. Their position changes throughout the night and from season to season. The experienced traveler recognizes and understands important stars and constellations wherever he goes in the northern hemisphere. The night sky can still be a source of fascination to the modern wilderness traveler.

Local winds and their changing patterns can also indicate direction to the experienced traveler. With the exception of Utah's High Uintas, all major mountain ranges in North America trend north and south. A single state like Nevada has a hundred mountain ranges, all coursing north and south.

Another method for determining direction in the absence of a compass or map is to sharpen a stick and poke it into the ground. Mark the end of the shadow that the stick casts. Sit back and relax. In an hour or so carefully mark the end of where the shadow now falls. Draw a line between these two points. The line will scribe a rough east-west direction. If you are lost the advantage of this system is twofold. It provides orientation, and the time it takes to determine direction provides an opportunity for you to rest and calm down.

A modification of the shadow method also involves driving a stick into the ground, but this time angle the stick so it doesn't cast a shadow. The tip of the stick should be pointing directly at the sun. Wait a short time and a shadow will emerge as the earth turns. The shadow on the ground will be in a rough east-west direction.

Another directional method involves pointing the hour hand of a watch at the sun. North will be halfway between the hour hand and twelve. This method is subject to a great deal of error as one approaches the equator. The increasing popularity of digital watches brings another rather obvious problem.

Natural methods of determining directions have considerable problems and disadvantages, but they can be useful in an emergency, even though there is no adequate substitute for a good compass and map. In parts of the American Southwest, the large stubby barrel cactus, a common and predominant plant, nearly always leans south or southwest. A lone barrel cactus cannot provide an absolute assurance of the direction; however, several leaning barrel cactuses will help guide your travel.

In many heavily forested areas of the north woods which were logged many years ago, old stumps are abundant. Careful inspection of a stump will reveal that tree rings are thicker on the south side and thinner on the north side. The bark of many aspen and poplar trees also provides a directional indicator. It is lightest on the south side and darkest on the north side. Moss on trees in some locales is thickest or found only on the north side. Continue to check these indicators to maintain a constant direction of travel.

Some knowledge of geology is an excellent aid to minimizing problems when traveling cross country. It leads to understanding where you can find water, shelter, and even the location of certain edible plants. In a general sense, a ridgetop provides the best view of the surrounding countryside; the rock is strong but the exposure to cliffs and to dropoffs is great. A gully or couloir has fewer possibilities of falls, but is exposed to rockfall from above and avalanches in the winter.

The type of rock formation provides both a sense of history of the land itself and an understanding of the climbing and hiking conditions that you can expect. Granite, solid, rough, and beautifully textured, has few possibilities for rockfall; footholds may be small, but of the very best. Metamorphic rock, fired and pressed from deep within the earth, is often broken and complex. Slopes made of such rock, whether in the Olympics or the Canadian Rockies, have lots of debris from rapid weathering. Many of its crumbling faces and slopes present rockfall hazards.

Sedimentary rock comes in a variety of conditions, from loose, crumbling sandstones and shales to solid, formidable limestone. Usually this type of rock weathers relatively fast, but conditions vary. In the East and in humid climates, limestone is melted away by the eons of time and water, but in the arid West, limestone forms impressive ridges and cliffs and can take on a marbled appearance where water flows over it, becoming slick and dangerous. Usually it is a good rock to climb.

Volcanic rock, black and foreboding, also comes in a variety of forms. It may be rotten and crumbling or solid and impressive. Often volcanic flows form numerous caves which make ideal shelters. Early man and his arrowheads are often found in such niches. Surface water is often lacking in volcanic areas, because porous rock can swallow entire rivers. Locating an edge of a lava flow or a shift in the surface rock can lead to springs and abundant sources of water. Without such understanding, one might wander over the hot, black surface of lava flows looking in vain for cool water.

A highway, a railroad, a stream, or a range of mountains provides a wide, permanent base for orientation. The comfort of a secure baseline is obvious. It is a large target for the wilderness traveler. Should you become disoriented, you need only walk in the approximate direction to reach a prominent baseline. If the base is a cabin or a spring, or another small point, it is far easier to miss when you are just beginning wilderness routefinding.

A baseline is important because people have a natural tendency to veer to the left or right. Without some form of reorientation, you will naturally travel in a large circle. The reasons for this are several, but in part result from asymmetry in the human body. It is possible to deviate 1 mile laterally or sideways for every 3 miles of forward travel. Most people don't have an instinctive sense of direction. Limited research by the military has shown that blindfolded people tend to bear off a straight path and circle back on their own path. Usually they circle to the right. Because walking a straight line is a learned method of wilderness travel and a beginning hiker may veer several miles from his starting point, a baseline is helpful.

The rate of travel is another important dimension of wilderness routefinding. For example, if your objective is 10 miles away, you will need to know the approximate travel time. Understanding personal travel time and distance will help you to determine your wilderness position.

After some experience you will know your approximate walking speed. On level ground or on a good trail, most people can hike 2.5 to 4 miles (4 to 7 km.) per hour. Terrain conditions and elevation will affect your travel time. Most people in good condition can climb about 1,000 feet (300 meters) in elevation per hour. Once the trail is left behind, however, rock, brush or tree cover, and terrain factors must be considered.

A distant view can orient you and help you to anticipate problems ahead. In some terrain, such as steep slopes, distance is difficult to estimate. If your route takes you over a ridge or through a jumble of rock, look carefully for details and something to provide scale to the scene. Sometimes a ledge or cliff will be deceptive and far more difficult to climb over when you get close. Have alternative routes in mind if a problem develops. Keep checking the back trail and remember the route in case you have to backtrack. Don't stubbornly refuse to give up on a poor route. A park ranger once started on an easy hike in Arizona's Saguaro National Monument. He glanced at a long ridge of sandstone that capped the mountain ahead. Three hours later, scratched, dehydrated, and upset, he gave up the goal to reach the top. The sandstone cap, 25 to 30 feet high, was crumbling and dangerous. Repeated attempts through the sandstone cap failed, one by one. A fall into a nearby cactus convinced him, painfully, of the folly of stubbornly sticking to his chosen goal. The next time he did not glance so briefly at a distant ridge but carefully searched out a passable route.

It's a good practice to look back and note the landmarks you have passed. On the return trek, the features will be easier to remember. If you feel you may forget the turn route, mark the way with pieces of paper, bent bushes, branches, or rocks. One rock stacked on top of another is a useful and obvious trail marker. If you are lost, leave messages for searchers — on a branch, at an obvious place on a ridge, at the edge of a meadow. If paper is available, leave several messages along the way.

You can also mark a route periodically with an arrow stamped out in the snow or formed out of rocks. It may be useful to scratch an arrow or your initials on a lake shore or beside a stream in the sand. Some sandstone and other smooth rock also can be scratched or otherwise marked. Charcoal from a fire may be used to leave a message on a sheltered rock. Some cross-country skiers, starting into a remote area, initial their tracks in the snow. It's a good idea to leave a message on a vehicle if you cannot sign out at a ranger station. In all cases, someone should know where you are going and when you will return.

Streams and rivers, especially at high water, often are serious barriers to travel. Small streams may be forded on logs or by jumping from rock to rock. If a stream is too wide for this, look for a shallow crossing that is free of large or deep pools. Don't cross above rapids or waterfalls. A stout pole is very useful in crossing swift streams. Lean into the current using the pole as support. Move slowly and be sure of your footing. Crossing mountain streams with bare feet may save your boots but be hard on your feet. They may become numb, injured, or cut in crossing the stream without your becoming aware of it. Wear a

Tree Blaze

Grass

← Rocks →

pair of heavy socks. Some hikers carry a pair of light tennis shoes both for camp and for crossing streams.

When a large river may be crossed only by swimming, an air mattress, a pillow, or a small log can be a useful aid. Untie your pack and its waistband, if it has one, and wear it loosely on your shoulders. Don't tie a rope onto a person wading or swimming in deep, fast water, because the current will pull him under if he is tethered. The swimmer may also get tangled in the rope and be pulled under. Swimming for the bank is a far superior choice. If both ends of a long rope or climbing rope are securely tied at opposite sides of a river, a person can cross holding onto the rope.

Obviously, the first to cross, perhaps a strong swimmer, will have to secure the rope for others.

If you must ford a major stream, select a spot where the current will sweep you over to the other side. Ideally, the landing area on the far side downstream will be a gravel or sand beach. Avoid any crossing that will carry you into a high bank, cliffs, brush, or logs or that will lead you to rapids. If you are swept away, go through rapids on your back, feet first, if possible. Avoid "holes," or large bubbly areas, behind rocks, because, lacking the buoyancy to hold a body near the water surface, they may tend to hold you under. Crossing any mountain stream, even on the hottest of summer days, may result in hypothermia. Consider this constantly when crossing swift or large streams. The rapid chilling can deaden the mind and cool the body in a few minutes. In winter, smaller streams may be crossed on snow bridges, but they can collapse under a skier or snowshoer. Banks of snow also may collapse after being undercut by a hidden water current. Immersion in the cold water, combined with winter temperature, is almost certain to bring on hypothermia. You will have to build a fire, dry your clothes, and rewarm yourself.

Falling through ice can result in hypothermia, which begins in only a few minutes. Quickly break off as much ice toward shore as is possible, because the current or a warm spring may have weakened the ice where you fell through. Stronger ice may be only a few feet away. When the ice is strong enough to hold your weight, kick and squirm up onto the ice. Roll or carefully slide off the ice. Don't stand until you are safely off it or until you reach a spot that is firm. Quickly start a fire, change clothes, and treat yourself for hypothermia.

Bogs or quicksand may be present in some parts of the southeastern United States. Occasionally, quicksand may be encountered elsewhere. With a little experience, you can identify the sand that is "quick." Quicksand has a spring or flow of water that supports the sand. Careful observation will reveal the telltale signs of water oozing or flowing upward. Usually you can avoid such areas.

One of the many myths of wildlands is that a person will be sucked into bogs or quicksand. This is impossible. However, if you fight the sand or muck and get tired, your head will become buried. If you are caught in such an area, flatten out onto your back and slowly move back the way you came. In more watery muck that cannot support any weight, swim with a slow breast stroke. Sweep the muck slowly away from your face while stroking a way out of the mess. If you avoid panic and stay flat, you won't be drawn down into sand or muck. A struggle will tire you quickly and make extraction more difficult.

With experience, you may also learn not to trust signs always. Several years ago a back-country ranger in Yellowstone National Park was riding horseback to a patrol cabin he had never visited. He intended to spend several days patrolling in the cold fall weather for hunters who might stray into the park while stalking elk. Because all the cabins had maps, the ranger carelessly did not bother to take one. He checked the trail on the office map and set out at midday. Progress went as expected until he reached a sign, "Harebell Cabin — 3 miles." By then it was late afternoon and he was looking forward to a warm, comfortable evening in the patrol cabin. An hour and a half later, he hadn't reached it. Confident that he had traveled well over 3 miles, perhaps as much as 5, he backtracked and looked for a side trail that he might have missed. Starting again at the sign, he rode for almost two hours. Still he found no side trail or cabin. As the cold evening came and the sun set, he became more and more concerned. With no sleeping bag and little food or supplies, he was faced with a cold night — and a hungry one. Finally, pushing the horse hard up the trail in the fading light, well over 5 miles past the sign, he found the snug patrol cabin. It was located not 3 miles, but more than 6 miles, from the sign. The lesson was obvious — if he had carried a map, he would have known that the sign had been improperly located.

In Greek mythology Theseus found his way out of a labyrinth after he slew a monster, by carrying a thread with him and following the thin line to safety. Routefinding is the maintaining of a thread of recognition throughout a wilderness journey. The secret lies in closely observing nature. Just as a book is a mystery to a child, so is the wilderness to the inexperienced. But after the many signs of nature are studied and learned, many pleasant journeys are available.

8

Weather

Ben Franklin once wrote, "Some are weatherwise; some are otherwise." Many people, especially those who live close to the land, have been fascinated by the capricious changes in weather. Climate and weather have historically resulted in abundant food or famine for people around the world. Even today, weather can change a pleasant walk in the woods into a survival exercise. A hunter who has climbed a familiar ridge finds his route obscured by snow and plunges into the storm lost and confused. A sunny afternoon sailing trip outside the bay becomes a race for life at the approach of a storm. Not only farmers but outdoor people should be "weatherwise."

Microclimate, or the temperature and weather conditions close to the ground, is of special interest, since people spend most of their time there. The lowest layer of air is complicated because of wide variations in temperature. Surface temperature on a hot day might be 140°F (60°C) or more, but at 6 to 7 feet (2 meters) above the ground the temperature may be only 86°F (30°C). Once the sun sets, the ground cools faster than the air because it is a better conductor of heat. Therefore, at night the ground is colder than the air, especially under a clear, dry sky. On humid nights, the ground cools more slowly.

Temperature varies near the ground for other reasons. Dark surfaces are warmer than light-colored surfaces. Low areas and depressions cause night air to settle, creating spots 18°F (10°C) colder than at higher elevations. Oceans, lakes, even ponds retain heat and create warmer night temperatures near shore. The opposite is true during the day, especially in the spring when lakes are cold. Daytime temperatures may be 18°F (10°C) cooler on a beach compared to inland.

In addition to understanding microclimate, the ability to predict weather is an important survival tool. It is akin to knowing edible plants and understanding the life habits of a ground squirrel. The knowledge of weather brings new and enjoyable dimensions to every trip. The amateur forecaster can check the daily weather signs on his wilderness hike and match his judgment against the three-day forecast of the evening weatherman. When you recognize and understand the dynamic unfolding of stormy weather, you will not only change and adapt to the weather but appreciate its impact. Our moods and psychological outlook are related to weather patterns. All the world is interrelated by the natural environment, since the winds link the continents and seas.

If there were no sun or heat to change our atmosphere, there would be no changes in the weather. The sun is the giant ladle that stirs the earth's air and, in turn, brings the pleasures and surprises of weather. The air or atmosphere moderates daytime temperature when the sun is out and slows the heat loss at night. As most campers know, a clear night is colder than a cloudy night since clouds trap the sun's heat. For the same reason, a cloudy day brings softer snow for cross-country skiing than a clear day.

Air warmed by the sun expands; rising warm air is replaced by the colder air above. On a global scale, the tropical air of the equator is replaced by the colder air to the north and south; on a local basis, the convection of air causes valley winds to blow upslope during the day. At night, the winds blow down the mountainside. During the day, cool breezes blow in from the

Valley winds in daytime

Mountain breezes at night

Warm Air

Cold Air

Effect of Mountains

ocean to the warm land; at night the reverse happens. Winds blow from the cooler land to the relatively warmer sea. This movement of air, driven by the sun, creates winds on both a local and global scale. And once the winds flow, other changes in weather evolve.

Water evaporates from the land and oceans, literally millions of tons of water each day. The capacity of the air to hold water varies with temperature. Warmer air can hold more water than colder air. Moisture rising into the cooler air condenses into clouds. Air flow over colder mountain areas causes rain or snow to fall. The side of a mountain facing the prevailing wind will have more moisture and deeper snow than the lee side of a mountain. Many of the great deserts of the world are on the sheltered side of mountain ranges, in the rain shadow. Moisture is carried around the world, but fickle winds and irregular land combine to spread the rain and snow unevenly. Some lands lie flat and inviting to every passing cloud, while high mountains block other lands from invading moisture.

Air masses are vast bodies of air that may cover hundreds of thousands of square miles. Major air masses adopt the temperature and moisture of the land over which they form. Swept by several air masses, the North American continent has several definite major patterns of weather. An understanding of the major air masses helps one to anticipate weather changes when isolated from weather reports. Usually, the air masses from the

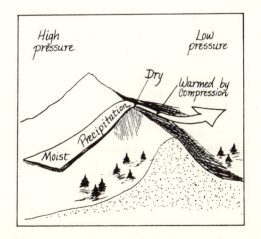

Mechanism of Chinook Winds

north are polar and the air masses from the south are tropical; both major bodies of air are modified if they flow from continental or maritime sources. Continental air masses are colder and drier; maritime sources are moist and warm. A continental air mass from the north is cold and dry. A polar storm that sweeps over the North Atlantic or Pacific is cold but moist; in the winter it may bring heavy snow or rain. Depending on the season of the year, the continent's major air masses follow fairly predictable routes once they break onto the land. The arrival of such air brings definite seasonal patterns of storms and weather.

Because of differences in temperature and humidity, major air masses do not mix well; instead, a boundary or front is formed. Usually, but not always, a front is pushed along an air mass. If a cold mass of air, continental in origin, pushes a warm front back it becomes a cold front. A warm mass of air that pushes cold air is called a warm front. Occasionally, the fronts may become stagnant or stationary and bring several days of mild rainy weather. Most of the time, fronts, unless they are weak, bring unsettled or bad weather. As with the movement of air masses, the pattern of frontal movement varies according to the season of the year.

As it advances, a cold front drives under warm air and usually brings a tower of clouds at the leading edge of the front. The speed of a cold front is fairly fast, 20 miles (33 km.) per hour or more during the winter months, when temperature differences are greater and pressures are higher. A barometer will drop rapidly with the arrival of a cold front.

A warm front pushes out colder air, and because warm air rises, the edge of a warm front rides up over the colder air it is replacing. The speed of a warm front is slower than a cold one, usually about half as fast. Often, precipitation falls at the leading edge of a warm front, but the amount of moisture decreases as the front passes. The movement and collision of large masses of air are major directors of weather, yet other influences are important, too. Mountains, lakes, and the sea all direct the weather — even cities moderate the winter's cold.

The cooling of air to its dew point, or saturation point, produces clouds. Those clouds produced near the ground usually are caused by the cooling of air. But the most rapid method of

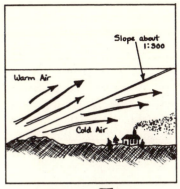

Warm Front

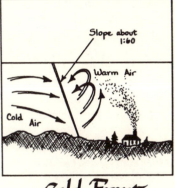

Cold Front

producing clouds comes from rising air. For example, fog and light drizzles result from low clouds, but thick, precipitating clouds are always a result of upward air movements.

Many types of clouds are produced by the lifting of air. The most common cause of lifting is the flow of air over mountains. Clouds are classified by altitude and type. The movement of air aloft and possible changes in weather are explained by the types of clouds created. Additionally, the sequence and pattern of clouds are important to predict and anticipate weather changes.

Under some conditions, the rapid lifting of moist, warm air results in a thunderstorm, one of the most dramatic cloud formations. A full-grown thunderstorm is an impressive sight. Clouds may tower 5 – 10 miles (8 – 16 km.) high and be capped with a short white anvil-shaped cloud. Lightning and thunder occur during the life of a thunderstorm. Lightning is simply a giant electric spark jumping between clouds or between the ground and clouds.

For mountaineers and boaters, the major hazard of a thunderstorm is the danger of lightning. Thunderstorm clouds can usually be seen for a considerable time prior to their arrival. Occasionally, a storm may break without warning onto climbers, if a mountain has blocked their vision. The sound of thunder usually warns of an approaching storm. The distance from lightning can be easily calculated by counting the seconds it takes for the thunder to reach after the lightning is seen. Counting at a normal speed in thousands will give the approximate seconds it takes for the sound to travel to you. Allow five seconds for each mile (four for each kilometer) from the strike.

Lightning causes the most fatalities of any type of storm. A 34-year record of storm deaths recorded an average of more than two hundred ligntning deaths each year in the United States. Many of these are boaters, hikers, climbers, and swimmers. Lightning also starts several thousand forest fires every year.

Another potentially dangerous product of a thunderstorm is hail, or balls of ice. Hailstorms grow as supercooled water droplets strike an ice pellet which has formed around a speck of dust. Hailstones grow in size as they are held in a thundercloud by powerful updrafts; sometimes they circulate through the cloud several times and can grow as large as baseballs. Hail is most noted for damaging crops, but a powerful storm can bring injuries, even fatalities, to people, if shelter is not available.

Tornadoes are the most sinister-looking and most violent storms. They are literally whirlpools of air that create the strongest winds known in the world. Winds of 270 miles (450 km.) per hour can develop within a storm. Forward tornado speed is much less, and the path of a tornado is narrow, usually less than a couple hundred yards. The typical funnel-shape cloud is its most distinctive feature.

Tornadoes are formed in advance of a cold front and are often accompanied by heavy rains and thunderstorms. More than 850 tornadoes strike the United States every year, following a predictable pattern. Although they occur more frequently in Texas, Oklahoma, eastern Kansas, and Nebraska than anywhere else in the world, they are also found elsewhere in the Midwest and in the southeastern United States. Tornadoes seldom occur west of the Rockies. They are preceded by an unearthly stillness in the air and by the formation of distinctive, extremely turbulent clouds in the sky. Experienced Midwesterners look for tornadoes in spring and summer and recognize the typical development of conditions that precede a storm.

The violent updrafts of tornadoes can suck debris, animals, and even houses into the air. The extreme low pressure at the center or vortex of a storm can cause barns and houses to explode as the vacuum passes over them. An average of over 130 people are killed each year by tornadoes in the United States.

The path of a tornado usually brings the storm out of the southwest and causes it to travel in a northeasterly direction. Although there are exceptions to this, you can travel at a right angle to a tornado and often escape its destructive force. If a storm is approaching, seek shelter in a ditch or even a small depression. Open areas or ditches are better locations to weather the storm than houses or cars, where flying glass and debris is especially dangerous. If caught on a lake with an approaching tornado, head for shore as fast as possible and always travel at an angle to the storm as on land; usually this will be in an easterly or westerly direction.

A hurricane or typhoon, the most feared of storms, has a far more widespread pattern than a tornado. A large low pressure area, about 500 miles (800 km.) in diameter, a hurricane differs from a frontal low in intensity, because it forms an almost perfect circle, and because it moves rather slowly through air masses of uniform temperature instead of along two different air masses of different temperatures.

Hurricanes develop only over open oceans with extremely warm, moist air masses and may last three weeks. They break up over land but may bring destructive winds and floods. Most that hit the United States sweep over the West Indies and strike the southeastern coast of the country.

Although weather forecasts over the radio give continuous warning and explanation on the development of tropical storms that may grow into hurricanes, it is worthwhile to understand traditional methods of predicting the arrival of a storm. An early indication is a wind from an unusual direction, such as the replacement of the normal flow of the trade winds from a direction other than east. Another clue is the arrival of high feathery

Cirrus

Cumulonimbus

Cumulus

Stratus

Cloud Masses

cirrus clouds or "mare's-tails." At sea, the arrival of high waves and swells, especially from an unusual direction, may give some warning. Such swells are traveling faster than the storm itself and may give several days warning. The time between waves changes from a gentle 4-to-6-second cycle to a 10-to-12-second pattern, and the surf begins to pound ominously.

A falling barometer is an obvious but not always early warning. In some cases the drop will occur twelve hours or less before a storm, and the distinctive rapid drop in pressure will occur only when the winds have started to blow. However, the top of a storm, sometimes reaching 30,000 feet or 10 km. high, may be seen as a bar near the horizon when it is 240 miles (400 km.) distant.

Hurricane winds are extremely destructive. A wind of 30 to 35 knots will blow off garbage can lids and even break some tree branches. Winds of 100 knots, not unusual in a hurricane, have nine times the pressure of a 35-knot wind. At 130 knots, wind pressure is sixteen times as great. At such pressure, large trees can be blown over, small buildings and mobile homes destroyed. Gusts in such storms can be higher and even more destructive. In the northern hemisphere the winds move counterclockwise around the center of the storm; the opposite is true in the southern oceans. Like a floor polisher, the revolving winds are fast, while the storm itself, like the body of the floor polisher, moves much slower from 10 to 50 knots.

In the Atlantic, the usual hurricane storm tracks are well known, but hurricanes are far from typical. Although an average of nearly ten storms develop each year and only two of them reach the shores of the United States, the actual number of storms varies greatly from year to year. They have occurred during all months of the year, but commonly they appear between June and November.

Along coasts hurricane damage is magnified by tidal waves or storm surges. The wind from a hurricane will keep the tide artificially high in bays and inlets. The low barometric pressure beneath such storms compounds the problem. A drop of one inch of mercury in a barometer will raise the sea level a foot. In a major storm the sea will rise several feet because of low pressure. If the storm coincides with a normal high tide, the potential for flooding is great. Under these conditions the storm surge may be 9 – 11 feet (3 – 4 meters) above normal high tide. The powerful storm that hit Galveston, Texas, in 1900 crested tides 15 feet (5 meters) above normal. Most of the 6,000 victims drowned. In August 1969, Hurricane Camille hit the coast of Louisiana and Mississippi with a 24-foot (7.5-meter) storm surge. It killed 135 people and left a billion dollars in damage in Mississippi alone.

Associated with hurricanes are torrential rains. When a storm passes over land it quickly diminishes in strength, but still can dump 10 to 12 inches of rain in a single day. Backpackers in the Smoky Mountains during Camille were hit with intense rainfall associated with the hurricane. Up to 25 inches (64 cm.) of rain fell in the mountain regions. Flooding in Virginia from the hurricane cost 112 lives.

Developing some skill at forecasting weather is one of the many pleasures of understanding the natural world. Prior to venturing into a wilderness or onto the sea, you should check the weather forecasts. The weather encountered a week from now is born today in the major air masses over the polar regions and oceans. Satellite images and modern communications can give you a better understanding and warning of pending storms prior to your departing on a venture. Keeping records at home with a small barometer and thermometer, and noting relative humidity, wind speed, and direction can lead to greater understanding of weather patterns. In any area, the local behavior of the weather is influenced by lakes, mountains, or even cities. Seasonal weather patterns will in turn influence the larger continental weather forces. There is no substitute for appreciating local conditions and the experience that comes with studying and understanding weather. But always remember, the most experienced meteorologist is surprised by sudden, unpredictable weather changes. Part of the joy of the wilderness is the exhilaration of a surprise storm.

The surprise of a storm should always bring a reminder of the basics of survival. The first and highest priority of any person caught in a storm is to seek shelter. A storm at sea in a small craft means a run for the nearest port, or failing that, the mustering of all possible seamanship. A mountain storm usually means a dash for shelter to avoid the wind, cold, and rain. Often a mountain storm means a rapid retreat down the hillside to avoid lightning, colder temperatures, and higher winds. In the winter, a storm will also mean avoiding the wind chill and often burrowing into the snow to find protection. A desert wind storm will bring the same search for shelter — this time to escape the blinding dust and sand. Once a safe and quiet shelter is found, you can reflect on improving your weather predicting ability.

For wilderness travelers or sailors, some forecasting can be done from the use of weather signs. Much of the interpretation of weather signs comes from the lore of sailors, farmers, and others directly affected by changes in the weather. One old saying is that a ring around the moon means rain. That observation alone is accurate roughly half the time. However, to observe a falling barometer and a ring around the moon at the same time raises the possibility of rain to 75%. Fair weather is commonly forecast when soft, billowing cumulus clouds dot the afternoon sky. Yet these same clouds may grow tall and dark in the afternoon and change the forecast to rain or thunderstorms. A steady or rising barometer usually means continued fair and clear weather. A rapidly rising barometer usually brings clear weather, although it might be storming at the moment of observation. A gentle wind from the west or northwest usually will continue a pattern of good weather.

Storms are often preceded by high thin cirrus clouds arriving from the west. When these thicken and are obscured by lower clouds, the chances increase for the arrival of rain or snow. Of course, a falling barometer usually brings stormy weather, as does a shift of wind from the north to west or southwest. The old saying "Red skies at night, sailor delight, red skies at morning, sailor takes warning" has validity. The morning sun turning the western sky crimson often signals the arrival of stormy weather. As the storm moves east, clouds may turn red as a clearing western sky opens for the setting sun.

A clear night sky brings cooler temperatures, while clouds, especially with a wind from the south, bring warmer temperatures. In mountain regions, the development of a cloud cap or lenticular-shaped cloud on tall mountain peaks is a weather indicator. A cap increasing in size or dropping lower in elevation signals the arrival of bad weather. A shrinking cloud cap indicates drier air, and better weather can be expected.

A cold front arriving in the mountains during the summer usually means several hours of rain and thunderstorms. Temperatures will drop 10°F or more for several hours. However, after the passing of a cold front, several days of clear, dry weather can be expected, since the cold front is dry.

Other weather clues are less precise, but useful in the wilderness. A morning rainbow is often followed by a squall. A midday rainbow means unsettled weather, while an evening rainbow marks a passing storm. A faint rainbow around the sun, often called a sundog, precedes colder weather. A midwinter sundog is often followed by some of the season's coldest weather. Smoke from a campfire can also help indicate barometric pressure. A rising column of smoke from a fire usually indicates a high pressure pattern and fair weather. But when your campfire smoke hugs the ground, a low pressure system is near and rain or snow can be expected.

Many people with old injuries or joints made sensitive by years of experience can "feel" the approach of a storm. Others conditioned to subtle changes in smell can sense the moisture and arrival of a low pressure system. Even birds can help predict the weather. Waterbirds fly low, scudding across the water, before an approaching storm. Fair weather finds them flying higher in the sky. Some experienced people maintain that the day's weather, fair or foul, is told from the songs of meadowlarks and mourning doves. Science probably does not support this idea, but solitary notes of a dove seem to be more pronounced before a storm.

The best way to improve weather predictions is to do some homework. Find a good elementary book on weather and climate. Watch the weather forecasts on the arrival of fronts and major masses of air. Observe changes in wind, temperature, humidity, and barometric pressure from the comfort of home. Keen observation coupled with homework will help develop some basic weather forecasting rules applicable to your particular area. Even a vacation in a new area can bring the opportunity to learn about new and different patterns. It is a simple matter to learn that the Colorado Rockies can expect forty to fifty days of summer thunderstorms and that the Cascades average fewer than ten storms during the summer months.

A simple barometer and wind direction observation can add considerable accuracy to anyone's forecasts. Although local conditions will vary, the table on page 131 is a basic start on personal forecasting.

All weather patterns are not predictable. The most highly trained and experienced forecasters are not always right. Standard weather bureau forecasts are accurate 80% to 90% of the time. Still, the excitement of nature lies partly in the surprises of weather that can be thrown your way. Your own challenge is to learn the predictable patterns of weather and apply your own experience and intelligence to second-guessing the workings of the large air masses and their personal impact.

Barometric pressure	Wind direction	Forecast
29.80 or less — rapid fall	N to E	"Nor'easter" gale due in hours. Snow or heavy rain continuing.
29.80 or less — rapid fall	E to S	Severe storm due in hours, then clearing.
29.80 or less — rapid rise	Moving to W	Storm ending, clearing and colder.
30.00 or less — rapid fall	NE to SE	Rain with high winds, then clearing within 35 hours.
30.00 or less — slow fall	NE to SE	Rain continuing.
30.00 or less — slow rise	SW to S	Clearing within hours, then fair weather for days.
30.10 or more — rapid fall	NE to E	Rain or snow in 12 to 14 hours.
30.10 or more — slow fall	NE to E	Rain in 2 to 4 days or in winter snow within 24 hours.
30.10 – 30.20 — rapid fall	NE to SE	Rain in 12 hours with wind.
30.10 – 30.20 — slow fall	NE to SE	Rain in more than 12 hours with wind.
30.10 – 30.20 — rapid fall	SE to S	Rain in 12 hours with wind.
30.10 – 30.20 — slow fall	SE to S	Rain in 24 hours.
30.10 – 30.20 — rapid rise	NW to SW	Fair with rain in 48 hours.
30.10 – 30.20 — steady	NW to SW	Fair for 24 to 48 hours.
30.20 or more — slow fall	NW to SW	Fair and warmer for 48 hours.
30.20 or more — steady	NW to SW	Fair.

9

Desert Survival

Deserts provide some of the best wilderness experiences and, during cool times of the year, some of the best opportunities for solitude and close encounters with nature. In the daytime the desert seems to be void of life. Yet to sit by a desert spring after a hot summer day is a stunning experience. For out of the void many animals — peccaries, deer, coyotes, bobcats, and others — come to drink. Yet during the day they are hidden away from the sun and people.

Desert travel can be safe and exceedingly interesting. Yet over the years, many thousands of people have perished in deserts. Desert wandering without water can be quickly fatal. You might last a month without food, but under the desert summer heat, with no protection and no water, you might die quickly and painfully. If you started walking at mid-morning under the desert's summer sun with no water, you'd be likely to perish before the day was out. If you sat in the shade or in a shelter during the summer heat and merely waited, without water you'd be likely to perish within two days.

On any wilderness trip several essential items should be taken along (discussed in Chapter 12), but for a desert trip some additional survival items may be helpful. A mirror for signaling and a magnifying lens for starting a fire are two examples of especially useful equipment. Take along water purification tablets, since sparse water supplies in the desert may be polluted by livestock and wildlife. A roll of linen thread, fine wire, or fishing line can be used in constructing shelters out of shrubs and bushes for protection from the sun, and in snaring rabbits, ground squirrels, and other animals in an emergency. Above all, carry along abundant water, and use it whenever you are thirsty.

Wear a cheap straw hat to keep your head cooler, to protect your eyes and shade you during the heat of the day. Long trousers and a long-sleeved shirt, if they are lightweight, loose fitting, and light colored, provide the best protection from the desert sun. Yet some people go into the desert wearing only shorts and T-shirts, although dehydration is accelerated by exposed skin, and many desert plants, with their thorns and spikes, can cause abrasions, cuts, and scratches. One casual stumble into a choya cactus can provide a painful and obvious lesson on the need for wearing boots in the desert. Yet many desert hikers travel in running shoes or tennis shoes. A pair of sturdy hiking shoes is essential for desert travel. Blisters on the feet are an unpleasant reality of desert travel. A change of socks will help alleviate this problem, but be sure to carry a needle to help relieve pressure from the fluid.

Always inform someone of where you are going and when you are expected back before you head into the desert. Plan your trip carefully and make a schedule. During the warmest weather don't attempt to hike during the heat of the day. Travel in the early evenings, in the mornings, or even at night, if possible, to avoid the debilitating sun. In the more benign mountain wilderness, if you are lost, you can afford to wander and look for other people, landmarks, or a way out. But if you are lost in the desert, you must exercise maximum self-control. Sit down and think very carefully — you cannot wander aimlessly in the desert. The miles that you can walk without water are few, and you cannot afford to miss a water source or waste energy and fluid. The desert can also be hazardous to the unprepared.

Of the several health hazards to keep in mind the most obvious is sunburn. Springtime hikers in the desert are especially susceptible to exposure from the sun and should wear long-sleeved shirts to cover exposed portions of the body even before redness and other obvious signs of sunburn occur. The drying nature of desert air makes it important to carry protection for the lips and skin to prevent chapping, drying, and cracking, as well as sunburn.

Whenever you venture into a warm environment, your body must dissipate heat to the surrounding air. The complex physiological response that cools your body, especially when combined with hiking or other activities, places extra demands on your system. Several heat-related problems can arise. Your legs, arms, or even abdominal muscles will have painful spasms — often as a result of salt depletion. Once the salt is replaced, especially with special salt and glucose drinks such as Gatorade or ERG, the problem quickly disappears. After a strenuous hike, keep some water and salt tablets near your bedroll in case cramps or thirst should keep you awake.

Heat exhaustion, a common heat problem, occurs in mountains or in the desert. The most common symptoms are extreme fatigue, giddiness, nausea, headache — and sometimes fainting. The pulse is weak and the skin clammy and moist — important signs. Treatment involves rest in a cool area and frequent drinks of water. Salt tablets or electrolyte-glucose drinks are especially beneficial. Recovery will normally be rapid.

A far more serious heat problem is heat stroke, a life-threatening emergency, which is technically named hyperthermia — the opposite of hypothermia. The body temperature rises rapidly to 106°F (41°C) or more. Lips may become blue, and the victim becomes confused or delirious. Often the skin is hot and dry, because sweating has ceased. Eventually heat stroke brings unconsciousness and convulsions, and if not treated immediately, heat stroke is fatal. The victim must be cooled rapidly. If possible immerse him in cool water and massage vigorously. If that is not possible, soak the skin and clothing with water and rapidly fan. Once the temperature begins to drop, stop the cooling process to avoid shock. Heat stroke treated in the field will then require medical attention.

To avoid problems of heat stress, maintain good physical condition and acclimatize yourself in advance to hot conditions. For ten days prior to a desert or warm-weather trip, run or work out in the sun for an hour or two each day. Dress in whatever is appropriate for the weather conditions at the time, wear a hat, and when temperatures are above 95°F (35°C), always wear light-colored clothing. Drink alcohol moderately, because it causes excessive water loss. Drink plenty of water periodically and don't wait until you are thirsty or dehydrated. Use salt tablets to help relieve sore muscles. Maintain an easy pace on any desert trip and don't get overheated.

If water is scarce, some things can help minimize your need for it. Keep your food intake at a minimum, for it takes extra moisture and fluids to digest food — more for protein digestion than for carbohydrates. Rest not only in the shade but, if possible, also elevated a few inches above the ground, since the earth may be 30°F or more warmer. Small gains in water conservation can be achieved by keeping your mouth shut. Breathe through your nose to reduce water loss by respiration. Pebbles in your mouth may help relieve some symptoms of water loss for a short while, but of course they add nothing to your water supply.

Keep a lookout for desert trails that fan out from waterholes. The white-winged dove and other birds in the American Southwest fly away from water in the morning hours and toward water in the evening. Animals such as the peccary root and dig for water where it is just below the surface. Sometimes it is possible to dig down 3 to 6 feet (1 to 2 meters) and find water in dry streambeds. A desert survival kit should include enough clear plastic and other equipment for making three or four solar stills. The presence of cottonwood, willow, salt cedar, cattails, arrowweed, and other indicator plants indicates subsurface water.

The desert has some unique foods. You need only observe animal droppings along desert trails to realize how important cactus is as a food supply. Virtually all cactus fruits are edible. Singe them over a fire to remove their tiny spines, then peel and eat them for their sugar. Their nuts are a good source of protein.

Even rattlesnakes are an excellent supply of food. However, kill a rattlesnake only if your dwindling food supply requires it and never just for sport.

There are two basic types of desert snakes: coral snakes and rattlesnakes. The coral snake, a slow, quiet, stunningly beautiful snake with red and black bands, has poisonous fangs in the rear of its mouth. It is very reclusive, and you will be bitten only if you are carelessly handling it, since it can envenomate only by chewing the venom into a victim. Its poison is neurotoxic, which means that it primarily affects the nerve function. The first-aid treatment for a coral bite is very different from that for a rattlesnake bite, which contains hemolysin, or a blood-destroying poison.

There are approximately thirty species of rattlesnakes, and although they exist in many areas, most species live in deserts. Rattlesnakes hunt primarily at night with a system of heat-sensing devices on their heads. They strike quickly and inject poison into their warm-blooded victims — fatal to small animals. All rattlesnakes are poisonous and all bites should be considered seriously.

Where does one find snakes? Snake dens are usually on the south sides of hills in rocky areas where the rocks act as thermal storehouses, holding the desert heat at night and during the winter. Snakes sometimes seek water for comfort when they are shedding their skin. They also seek animals attracted to water. Although rattlesnakes are not aggressive and will not chase you, be careful around water, near rocks, in brush — the sorts of places that you will naturally seek out for shade and shelter. Rattlesnakes cannot tolerate the extreme heat of the desert floor and seek the shade during the daytime.

You can take several precautions to avoid rattlesnake confrontations when you are hiking in the desert. Wear protective clothing, boots, and full-length pants, especially in the evening when snakes are on the move. Always watch where you put your hands and feet. Over 90% of snake bites occur on the extremities. Walk in open areas and be extra careful when stepping over rocks or debris that may shelter a snake. If you must leave camp at night, use a flashlight. Also when gathering firewood, check the surroundings and watch for snakes.

Snakes don't always rattle before striking, but a rattle is a good warning. If you hear a snake, freeze until it is located; then make a slow and calm retreat. Although some people state that a snake can strike only a half or a third of its body length, the western diamondback, without being coiled, can strike the full length of its body and, in some cases, will actually leave the ground while striking. If you have never heard a rattlesnake, the sudden buzz of one close at hand will leave no doubt as to what it is. Your instinct will be to jump, but don't fall down or frighten the snake into striking. It won't chase you, so self-control and slow movement are the best tactic. Teach children to respect snakes but not to have undue fear of them. Finally, don't kill desert animals unless it is essential to do so.

If you are bitten by a rattlesnake, arrange for first aid immediately because there can be damage not only to muscle tissue but to kidneys and brain as well. Loss of fingers, severe muscle damage, and other crippling injuries can occur. The main thing is to get the venom out of your system. A western diamondback, for example, can inject 250 mg. to 300 mg. of venom with one bite, but all it takes to kill a 170-pound man, if nothing is done to remove the venom, is about 150 mg. A few years ago the use of ice and cooling therapy was regarded as a good first-aid technique. In recent years, however, it has been rejected because of the additional problems that cold brings to the tissues. Although cold does slow down circulation, it also slows the body's defense mechanism against venom.

The first thing to do is to check and see if the snake has actually injected poison into your body. There will be at least one fang mark if it has, and swelling will occur within a few minutes or an hour. The bite will become very painful and discolored and shock may result. A rattlesnake bite may cause nausea, weakness, numbness, breathing problems, and even temporary blindness. As in most other cases of injury, fear and panic are the worst response. Exertion and excitement will only exaggerate the problem and may bring on shock. If you are bitten and still able, try to kill the snake and take the dead reptile to the hospital. Because different snakes have different types of venom, hospital treatment will vary with the species of snake.

Fang Marks

Incorrect
Incision

Correct
Incision
(shallow)

Snakebite Treatment

If the signs and symptoms indicate that a bite penetrated a person's skin and poison was injected, the first-aid procedure is: First, put the victim in a comfortable prone position. Second, if the bite is on an arm or leg, try to keep the extremity below the level of the heart. Apply a flat constricting bandage at least a half-inch wide. The bandage may be a belt, a handkerchief, a shirtsleeve, or whatever is available. The constricting bandage should be between the bite and the heart, approximately 2 to 3 inches above the bite. Always keep the bandage above the swelling, but don't use it if the bite is on the head or face. The bandage should be loose enough so that a finger can be inserted underneath it without much effort. You should be able to feel a pulse below it. A tourniquet or a bandage that is too tight will cut off blood circulation, with undesirable results. Don't loosen the bandage every few minutes, as many books have shown in the past, and don't allow the swelling to reach the constricting bandage, but move the bandage higher if needed. If medical assistance is available in three to four hours, nothing else should be done. Always get a snakebite victim to a hospital as soon as possible.

If help is hours away, sterilize the wounds with an antiseptic or soap and water. With a sterilized scalpel or knife, make a straight incision that connects both fang marks and extends ¼ inch past each puncture. The cut should go through the skin and fat but not into muscles, tendons, or nerves. Under no circumstances should the cut go deeper than ¼ of an inch. Despite the instructions in old first-aid manuals, the incisions should never be cut in the shape of an X. Initially some honey-colored venom may be seen. Squeeze the venom, blood, and fluid gently from the incision with the fingers for 20 to 30 minutes or for as long as it takes to get the victim to a doctor. Don't use oral suction. The mouth contains a great deal of bacteria, and this can lead to serious infection of the bite region. If you carry antivenom on desert trips, it can be used in an emergency, but the instructions on each package must be followed rigidly. There must be a skin test for an allergy and that test must prove negative. Failure to do this can result in death by shock if the victim is subjected to an allergic reaction.

Initially, shock, pain, and fear are the most serious results of snakebite. A more serious problem is the risk of infection as well as serious muscle and nerve damage from the venom. The old cliché about alcohol or whisky being a snakebite-treatment technique is blatantly false, for the alcohol only increases the absorption of the venom in the bloodstream and should never be used. Certain pain-killing drugs such as demerol and morphine also increase the toxicity of the venom. If you plan extended desert trips, consider taking along antivenom kits which can be stored without losing their effectiveness for several years. Also carry detailed first-aid instructions and don't rely on tourniquet or cooling methods found in old survival manuals. The ice treatment or cooling treatment inhibits the action of natural enzymes that detoxify a portion of the rattlesnake venom. The cooling also impairs the blood supply and can result in seriously injured tissue and even gangrene.

The Gila monster, a colorful but homely-looking reptile, is one of the two venomous lizards in the world. It is also rare and endangered. Few people are bitten by Gila monsters unless they are actually handling the animals. Although they do have venom, there is greater danger from their bacteria-infested mouths which can result in dangerous infection.

Scorpions, another desert creature that many people fear, are widespread outside the desert regions as well. Usually nocturnal, they are found under rocks and dead logs or among shrubs and bushes. Avoiding scorpions is the best defense. Take care when you sit down. Don't put your hands where you can't see — for example, when gathering firewood or rocks for a campfire.

Scorpions require moisture and may be attracted to humid boots, a sweaty shirt, or a bedroll. Always shake out your clothing before you use it. Be especially careful at night, and don't walk barefoot in desert country.

A neurotoxin like a wasp or bee sting, scorpion's poison can be exceedingly painful, and little first aid can be done in field conditions. One genus (*Centravoides*) of desert scorpion is lethal. If the reaction to a scorpion sting is very strong, the victim may have to be treated for shock and taken to medical care as soon as possible. The lethal species is neither the largest nor the easiest to identify, and often the victim never sees the scorpion. But a strong reaction will require emergency treatment.

Constricting bandages, incisions, and the kind of first aid used for certain types of rattlesnake and black-widow bites are useless with scorpions stings. The amount of venom is minute and affects the nerves — treatment is very different. Some people may have an allergic reaction to a scorpion sting.

A scorpion sting produces a prickling sensation, and a heat-rash type of reaction may develop. The area affected may become quite sensitive. The victim may become exceedingly restless and jittery; in advanced stages, convulsions or respiratory difficulty may occur. The site of the sting may become very hard and abnormally sensitive. An antivenom available for scorpion stings is not usually used for adults, only for children. They often develop hives, considerable swelling, and tightness in the chest, nose, and throat within a few minutes of being stung. If antihistamines, such as allergy tablets, are available, they may be the most effective first-aid treatment. Rest, food, warmth, and fluids should be provided later on.

Small, reclusive scorpions are the most serious venomous desert creatures. One Mexican species, the Durango scorpion, is reported to have been responsible for more than 1,600 deaths in Durango over a 35-year period. In Arizona in recent decades, 68% of the deaths due to venomous animals were caused by scorpion stings.

The tarantula, a very formidable-looking desert creature, has starred in many horror movies. But those who have known the spider — John Muir, for example — insist that it makes a nice pet. Its hunting technique is primarily a mechanical biting action, and its bite is not poisonous to humans. Tarantulas are best observed, enjoyed, and allowed to go on their way.

The black-widow spider is another desert creature with a bad reputation. The female, a graceful black spider with a vivid red hourglass shape on the underside, is dangerous to man. Often the victim never sees the spider or blames it for the illness. Very reclusive, black-widow spiders live in the basements of houses, behind rock walls, and in other areas where they can hide easily. As indicated by a report, "Nearly half of the black-widow spider bites reported in medical literature in the first four decades of this century were inflicted by spiders lurking underneath the seats of outdoor toilets." The spider's bite can be fatal to older people in poor health and to children.

A person bitten by a black-widow feels a pain like a pinprick and a slight burning. After fifteen minutes or an hour, severe pain may develop around the area of the bite, spread throughout the body, and grow extremely severe until the victim writhes in agony. The abdominal muscles may become rigid, with heavy perspiration, dizziness, nausea, and vomiting following. Signs of shock are obvious. Breathing may become labored, speech blurred, and coordination impaired. The victim may appear to be intoxicated. Treatment includes painkillers, if available, but not the incision-and-suction method, which is useless and merely increases the danger of infection. The pain usually disappears after two to four days, but recovery may take two weeks. Sometimes local infection occurs around the bite, and the skin sloughs off until a small cavity remains.

Desert mirages are a phenomenon almost as old as ancient history. They are mentioned in the Koran, and were known to the Arabs at least fourteen hundred years ago. Mirages have been the sources of many illusions, but they are physical realities, a result of bending light by refraction. They occur not only in deserts, but wherever air temperture differences exist. A distant mountain range viewed through a warm air inversion looms larger than reality. A "water" mirage on the hot desert is actually a reflection of the sky, a result of the light bent upward. Mirages are caused by different densities in layers of air that are close to the earth's surface. The light rays reaching your eyes travel by several paths through these different densities of air and produce the distorted, multiple, sometimes even inverted scenes. To look through binoculars only magnifies this sense of strangeness. If a mirage blocks your view, there is little that you can do except hike to a higher point or a ridgetop to look down across the valleys and open areas. A mirage is not a result of dehydration, but a person strained by thirst may misinterpret the phenomenon.

Safe and pleasant travel in the desert holds still other considerations. During the summer months in the Southwest, for example, you must keep looking at the sky for signs of impending thunderstorms. Even though the sun is shining and no rain is falling, thunderstorms in the distant mountains can result in a flash flood where you are. Dry stream beds, known as washes or arroyos, with their soft sand, make attractive camping places, and during the winter months, when there is only a remote chance of thunderstorm, they may be acceptable camping areas. During the summer, they are not. If a flash flood does occur, don't try to cross a wash. Organ Pipe Cactus National Monument in southern Arizona, a beautiful desert wilderness park with an area of 500 square miles, has only two small sources of permanent water. Despite this, one of the early fatalities in the park occurred by drowning. An impatient prospector, faced with a flooding arroyo, chose to try to wade across it and was swept away by the flood and drowned — ironically in one of the driest areas in the United States.

Dust storms are another problem in desert areas. If you are driving in a dust or sand storm, you should pull off the road in a safe area and avoid the risk of driving until the storm passes. If you are on foot, seek shelter behind rocks, in gullies, wherever you can avoid the dust.

If your desert hiking or camping trip requires a long drive through remote country, see to it that your motor vehicle is in good condition, with a good battery, hoses, spare tires, spare fan belts, necessary tools, and reserve oil and gasoline. It is also a good idea to carry extra water for the radiator. Going into the desert in an automobile requires special equipment. Take a shovel or two, a tire pump, an axe to cut brush and shrubs, but most important, extra water — 5 gallons (20 liters) for each person for each day of desert travel. Go slowly on back roads. Get out and check sandy areas and dry stream crossings; they may be easy to traverse one day yet soft and hazardous the next. Experienced travelers carry large planks in their trucks for crossing these sandy areas. A ship's anchor tied to the front bumper winch of a four-wheel-drive vehicle is a sure sign of an experienced desert traveler. He understands that he is most apt to become bogged down in the wide desert washes full of sand and rocks. How is an anchor used? Walk out in front of a mired vehicle, pulling the anchor and cable from the winch. Drop the anchor in the sand and winch the vehicle up to the anchor. With a few repetitions, the widest desert wash can be crossed relatively easily.

A ship's anchor is not the only incongruous but useful desert adaptation. When United States Army troops pursued renegade Apaches in the late 1880s, they faced very tough and hostile foes who were adapted to the desert environment. The army had one advantage, however. Its heliograph stations based on desert mountain peaks in Arizona and New Mexico signaled troops miles ahead to coordinate the pursuit of small Indian bands. It was the army's very practical adaptation to the desert environment that resulted in Cochise and other Apaches being driven into Mexico and their eventual capture. Today, with many days of sunshine, a small pocket mirror can be an effective signaling tool at 10 miles or more.

If you are stalled or lost, prepare a smoky signal fire in the daytime and a bright one at night. Three fires in a triangle will signal that help is needed. Signal fires are fairly easy to make. The harshest North American desert contains shrubs, bushes, and grasses that can be gathered, piled up, and, because they are usually dry, quickly built into a fire to signal aircraft or distant people. Brush can also be piled in the shape of an X or SOS. If placed in open areas they can be seen from passing aircraft. During the morning and evening hours the brush will cast shadows easily visible from a plane.

Generally, if your vehicle breaks down, stay near it. Your emergency supplies are there, the vehicle can be seen for miles, and you should have an adequate water supply for several days. The vehicle has things that can be used in survival, mirrors to flash a signal at aircraft, or a spare tire to burn for a signal. Hubcaps can be used for collecting water in a solar still. If the car is bogged down or stranded, you can pull out the seats to rest off the hot desert floor. Shade can be created from tarps, blankets, seat covers — whatever will reduce the rays of the sun.

If you have to leave a disabled vehicle, do so only if you are positive of your route to help and completely confident that you can reach water or assistance. Roads are signs of civilization; it is usually best to stay on one. Don't wander into the desert in an aimless search for water or help. Never leave during the hottest time of day. Be sure to leave a note telling what time you left and the direction in which you are planning to travel. A small pad of cigarette papers may be useful for leaving notes on cactus and shrubs or merely to mark a trail through the desert. Mark your route periodically with small bits of paper, rags, rocks, or arrows scratched in the soil. Searchers will be able to follow your route if it is well marked. If you must walk, rest for at least ten minutes out of every hour — in the shade, if possible. If you are in poor physical condition, rest more frequently and for longer periods. If you have water, be sure to drink it — never ration it. Drink whenever you are thirsty, even if that means exhausting the supply. You will live longer that way than if you try to hoard water to make it last. Many people have been found dead of dehydration in desert areas with water still in their canteens. If your water supply is short, avoid unnecessary talk and eat only very small amounts, if at all. Don't smoke or drink alcohol, and avoid salts and spices. Most important, keep your clothing on. It will help to keep your body temperature down and reduce the rate of dehydration by making your sweat work efficiently to cool your body. Be sure to cover your head. If a hat is not available, improvise a head covering.

For those who love and appreciate the desert, experiencing the gamut of its unique offerings can be pleasant and rewarding with the proper preparation, planning, and understanding of the limits due to heat and the absence of water. Joseph Wood Krutch, a New Yorker transplanted to the Southwest desert country, wrote of the mystical overtones the desert held for him. Many others have delighted in the desert and in Krutch's eloquent description of its phenomena. Desert travel, for those who are prepared, holds some of the most memorable wilderness experiences.

10

Mountain Survival

Mountains have evolved not only their own epics and heroes, but even a literature of their own. Only the sea can claim a wider audience of more popular writings. Mountains have lured people to adventure and enthralling survival experiences since even before the days of European alpinists. Mountaineers climb to find beauty and themselves; they risk mountain storms, rockfalls, avalanches, and lightning strikes in part as a test of their own will. Survival anecdotes and climbing stories go hand in hand.

At higher elevations, hikers and climbers experience a loss of appetite, and the attraction of sugar diminishes. Above 14,000 feet (4,100 meters), lack of oxygen makes it difficult for the body to process and utilize fatty foods, and many people cannot digest fats. Because of this, mountaineers must change their diets to include more carbohydrates like rice, cereals, and sugar, as well as more protein like meats and dairy products. Mountain air is often very dry, and excessive panting from climbing dehydrates body tissue and increases water loss. Both food and water requirements change with stressful alpine conditions.

Mountaineering brings two unusual medical problems. The first, mountain sickness, develops in some individuals at 7,000 or 8,000 feet (2,000 or 2,350 meters), and almost everyone is susceptible at elevations of about 12,000 feet (3,500 meters). Symptoms are exaggerated in those who live close to sea level and who travel into higher elevations. A person from San Francisco who climbs high in the Sierras for a weekend trip, or one from Portland or Seattle who climbs Mount Rainier or Mount Hood, is especially vulnerable. Symptoms of mountain sickness are drowsiness, a general sense of weakness, tiredness, and lack of energy. Because of a lack of oxygen, the face may take on a pallor; the lips and fingernails may have a bluish tinge. Uneasiness and headaches, even nausea, may be experienced. Avoid smoking, drinking alcohol, and heavy eating if mountain sickness symptoms develop. Since a person who suffers from mountain sickness often cannot sleep, it is a good idea to carry aspirin to relieve headaches and help to relax and get a good night's sleep.

The body begins to acclimatize immediately to higher elevations, but there is a limit to physical adjustment depending on individual health and physiology. For most people, the limit of acclimatization is around 18,000 feet (5,500 meters). Higher than that, the human body cannot acclimatize; lower it can. Most people become 90% acclimatized in ten days and 98% acclimatized in six weeks. The blood increases its ability to take on oxygen; the lungs are more efficient, and several physiological changes take place. (Conversely, acclimatization is lost at sea level in eight to ten days.) Organizers of successful mountaineering trips consider acclimatization and allow time for members of a party to adapt to alpine conditions. Not extremely serious in itself, mountain sickness does bring a great deal of discomfort.

High altitude pulmonary edema is a very serious problem. Some medical authorities regard it as an advanced stage of mountain sickness; and the dividing line between the two is not entirely clear. Generally, pulmonary edema occurs at higher elevations than mountain sickness, usually above 9,000 feet (2,700 meters). Some individuals become acclimatized in one to three weeks and don't suffer from pulmonary edema; others cannot adjust to its unique problems. The symptoms are similar to those of pneumonia, and some mountain deaths, historically attributed to pneumonia, may actually have resulted from high altitude pulmonary edema. Basically, an accumulation of fluid in the lungs obstructs the flow of air and the exchange of gases in the lungs. Death results from suffocation or heart failure. For most people, the symptons of pulmonary edema occur 12 to 36 hours after arrival at a high elevation. The problem may start with shortness of breath, weakness, loss of appetite, nausea, and tightness in the chest. A cough begins to develop, usually becomes more persistent, and later produces a thin frothy sputum in which blood may or may not be present. Pulse and respiration increase and may become very rapid. The lips and fingernails turn blue because of the shortage of oxygen. If not treated and removed to a lower elevation, the victim suffers collapse, coma, and eventually death. In its advanced stages, pulmonary edema brings a bubbling sound in the chest, as the lung fluid gurgles with each passing breath. The victim often feels as if he is drowning — and he is. At a high elevation, oxygen may be administered, but there is no substitute for a rapid return to a lower elevation while the victim is still mobile. A drop of only 2,000 feet (600 meters) in elevation may restore normal breathing.

Since mountains tend to be wet, windy, and colder than the surrounding terrain, hypothermia is another problem associated with high elevations. In addition, those who travel into the mountains are rapidly expending energy and may be eating poorly, hence they become possible victims of hypothermia.

Prolonged exposure to cold, especially wind chill, can cause frostbite. One of the first signs is a lack of sensation in the face, fingers, or toes. The bright, healthy red skin associated with outdoor activity is replaced by white patches or a blotchy appearance. These areas become numb and the tissue hard or rubbery to the touch. Frostbite and a person's tendency to become frostbitten are enhanced by exhaustion, injury, disease, lack of adequate food, smoking, and consumption of alcohol. Risk is reduced by taking adequate vitamins, particulary the B complexes and vitamin C, good health, and, of course, good equipment and shelter.

During and after thawing, frostbite areas are extemely painful. Blisters may appear and the areas become black and blue because the cell walls under the skin have been broken down or damaged. These areas are like bruises where blood collects underneath the skin and turns a dark blue or black. Frostbite can be best prevented by wearing adequate clothes for protection from wind and cold. The wind-chill factor, rapid cooling at low temperatures from wind, must be especially avoided by wearing a face mask, scarves, and gloves. The best treatment is rapid rewarming, a technique usually not possible in the field. A person can walk out of a wilderness area with frozen toes or feet and then rapidly rewarm the frozen areas with water at a temperature of 108° – 112°F (42° – 44°C). Rapid rewarming minimizes the damage to the toes, feet, or hands, but painkillers and medical assistance also must be used because of the excruciating pain.

One of the most damaging of the many survival method claims that the treatment for frostbite is to rub the frozen area with snow. This is ludicrous because snow will only cool and freeze the area more and cause additional damage. Another misconception is that alcohol, such as rum or brandy, is a good treatment for frostbite. Although drinking alcohol gives the sensation of warming, it actually dilates the blood vessels and increases the loss of body heat.

Lightning strikes injure or kill many mountaineers. They are largely predictable, however, and, contrary to popular opinion, lightning almost always strikes areas twice or even more. During a thunderstorm, some areas are relatively safe and others are quite dangerous.

There are three types: (1) cloud-to-cloud lightning, (2) cloud-to-ground or downstroke lightning, and (3) ground-to-cloud or upstroke lighting. The first is usually harmless except for hang gliders and glider pilots. The second usually lasts only for a fraction of a second but is fatal about 30% of the time. The third variety lasts longer, the stroke is hotter — the temperature reaches 50,000°F (27,750°C) or higher — and it draws 100 to 300 amperes. If it passes through a human, an upstroke is almost always fatal. Victims are almost always burned. Cardiac arrest also occurs frequently. Respiration is often stopped, so the treatment includes both heart massage and mouth-to-mouth resuscitation. In mountains, however, many lightning casualties result not from a direct hit but from the fusion of voltage through the ground, called step voltage or ground shock. As might be expected, ground shock is most severe near the actual lightning strike and dissipates outward.

The most common targets are lone trees, the tallest trees in a forest, the tops of mountains, or the point of a cliff or ridge. (A boat on a lake or the mast of a ship at sea also is a prime target for lightning.) A cave that is damp or recessed below a ridge is also unsafe, largely through the danger of ground shock. Dry caves or areas between flat rocks are safer.

Lightning is a product of thunderstorms, which travel 25 mph or faster. At the approach of a storm, it is important to look for shelter. If you are caught in the open, stay away from climbing gear, pack frames, or any other metal objects. Crouch or lie down; don't stand up. Put a sleeping bag, a robe, or any other insulation between yourself and the ground. The use of insulation 4 inches (10 cm.) or more thick is often good protection from ground shock. As long as they don't touch any metal objects, fire lookouts in the high mountains of the West protect themselves, with no adverse reaction from lightning during a storm, by standing on an insulated stool with glass insulators instead of metal or wooden legs.

During a storm in the mountains, avoid streams, wet canyons, or couloirs, which are routes that transmit ground shock. Stay off a ledge or cliff, but it is safer to be out some distance from a point of rock rather than immediately beneath it.

Heart massage and mouth-to-mouth breathing can revive many lightning victims. Brain damage may occur and breathing may stop for up to 25 minutes before it resumes normally.

Broken bones, head injuries, and other problems sometimes occur from falls that take place after someone is struck by lightning. Burns, lacerations, internal injuries, and amnesia also commonly occur because of lightning strike or ground shock.

Every year approximately one thousand lightning injuries occur in the United States, with 250 to 300 deaths. Many of those who survive receive immediate emergency cardiac care, which plays a major role in the victims' recovery. Seemingly dead patients have recovered from the initial shock by prolonged cardiac pulmonary resuscitation. Although arresting of the heart and breathing is the most obvious result of being struck by lightning, there may be other serious wounds. There is often a depressed entrance-and-exit wound. The area around the wound may be charred and surrounded by a spider-like or zig-zag burn of varying degrees. As the lightning current penetrates the body, skin burns are followed by injury to deeper tissue. The severity of damage is difficult to determine in the field because of the unpredictable course the lightning track takes through the body. Although heart stoppage from the shock is the worst problem, there may be other signs of central nervous system damage such as respiratory arrest, unconsciousness, coma, disoriented behavior, hysteria, amnesia, or paralysis. The lungs and abdomen may swell with fluid and internal bleeding may occur. Violent muscle contractions, which may have started when the lightning struck, often cause the victim to fall and cause severe bone fractures or dislocated joints. As soon as the immediate problem of respiratory and cardiac arrest has been taken care of, the victim must be treated for shock, internal or external bleeding, open wounds, and back, neck, or bone injuries.

Avalanches are another major concern for those who venture into the mountains during the winter months. Knowledge of snow, although complex, can help you avoid being caught in a snow avalanche. Understanding avalanches can help you survive a slide if buried. But even experts who have studied snow avalanches for years don't fully understand the conditions that trigger them. Experience alone cannot prevent a person from being caught in an avalanche. Despite his experience, Willi Unsoeld, one of the most famous and experienced mountaineers in the world, and a party of students on a Mount Rainier expedition were caught in an avalanche in 1979. Before they could be rescued, he and a young student perished.

Because it is impossible to predict avalanche conditions with certainty, a skier or snowshoer can rely only on general guidelines. But as with most other aspects of wilderness survival, it is important to develop judgment and understanding of local snow conditions, to follow the snowfall pattern and development of the snowpack throughout the season, and, if there is any doubt, to stay out of snow avalanche areas.

There are two main types of snow avalanche. Loose-snow avalanches start at a single point or in a small area, and as they roll downhill, they grow in size and quantity of snow. Loose-snow avalanches develop when there is little internal cohesion and strength in the snow, usually after a fresh snowfall. Slab avalanches start when a large area of snow begins to slide at once. There is a well-defined line or fracture zone where the moving snow breaks away from the stable snow. This fracture line, depending on conditions, may be several feet high. Slab avalanches are characterized by the tendency of snow crystals to stick together; large angular blocks or chunks of snow may bunch together in the slide. Most avalanche victims are caught in slab avalanches. In many cases, the victim triggers the avalanche with his weight on the snow or with skis cutting across a slope.

Ground cover increases the hazards of snow. A slope with large rocks and trees helps anchor the snow. Smooth, grassy slopes or those with flexible shrubs and brush are more danger-

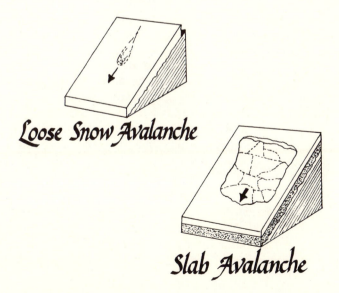

Loose Snow Avalanche

Slab Avalanche

ous. The snow slides easily on those slopes compared to a snow-pack anchored to a heavy stand of trees. Nevertheless, in the spring, after an unusually heavy year of snowfall, a hike in the mountains often reveals snowslides that have swept away large old stands of trees, sometimes smashing them like matchsticks because of the force of the slide. Under extreme conditions, even trees in heavy snowcover cannot prevent an avalanche from taking place.

Avalanches are found mostly on slopes of intermediate steepness (30° to 45°). The steepest slopes, of course, don't build up significant amounts of snowfall, because the snow sloughs off before dangerous avalanche conditions can occur. Gentler slopes can become hazardous if large avalanches sweep down from above or, under rare conditions, when the snow is deep and wet. But generally, slopes from 30° to 45° are the ones to avoid. Related to this is the profile of a slope. Although slab avalanches, the most dangerous, can sweep down concave slopes, generally the starting or most dangerous zone is the convex area of a slope.

Use short slopes, ones just a few yards long, to test avalanche conditions. Find a slope that is as steep as the surrounding hills, and ski onto it. Jump up and down to see if the snow will move. In testing a slope, be sure to consider the direction that it faces. During midwinter, south-facing slopes and those that face northeast or northwest are most apt to slide in midwinter. South-facing slopes are most dangerous in the spring or on sunny days when the snow warms and becomes very wet.

Slopes on the lee side of windblown ridges are another major worry for mountain travelers. Leeward slopes of a ridge or hill are particularly dangerous because wind-deposited snows are deep and create hard, hollow-sounding wind slabs. Windward slopes, those that face the direction of the wind, have less snow and are safer. A sustained wind of 15 mph rapidly increases avalanche danger, for the snow collects in large amounts at the deposition zone on the lee side of ridges and mountains. Such snow, disturbed by the wind, hardens in a process called age hardening. Wind is the biggest mover of snow, and often a careful observer can see a dull slab of snow that reflects less sunlight than fresh snow that has not been disturbed because the snow crystals that reflect light have been broken and rounded. Look for slabs on the lee side of ridges, but be careful. They are some of nature's most beautiful traps.

A snow plume on a ridge or a peak is a sign that dangerous conditions are developing. In many cities of the western United States, such as Denver, Reno, or Salt Lake City, a clear winter day will reveal a beautiful wispy plume of snow blowing off the ridges of the Rockies, the Sierras, or the Wasatch mountain ranges — beautiful to look at but a sign that dangerous slab-avalanche conditions are forming.

Old snow, as well as fresh snow, may contribute to avalanches. Frequently, an early winter storm that covers the mountains will lie on the surface of the ground, and in a complex process called constructive metamorphism, which apparently happens when water vapor moves through snow cover, ice crystals form. Far different from the original snow, these cup-shaped crystals are usually formed in the deepest few inches of snow, just above the ground, and are called depth hoar. In some conditions they form on top of an old layer of snow. They are easy to locate by shoving a stick or ski pole down through the snow. If the stick or ski pole suddenly breaks through a weak layer of snow below, it is a warning sign. Often a person can reach down and drag out a handful of these beautiful cup-shaped snow crystals. Unfortunately, they create a loose, precarious under-layer for the winter snows that follow. Once depth hoar conditions develop, they may last until spring. On any ski trip, check the snow profile and look for weak layers of snow or icy layers that create dangerous avalanche conditions.

Close to 80% of all avalanches occur during and after storms, when loose snow creates avalanche conditions. Often these storms are accompanied by winds that add to the seriousness of the avalanche potential. A period of good weather after such a storm tends to settle the snow and stabilize conditions. Stabilization occurs fairly rapidly the first day or two after a snowstorm. But be particularly cautious during and immediately after a storm that brings several feet of snow to the mountains.

Snowfall, at a rate of more than 1 inch an hour, rapidly increases avalanche danger, particularly if it continues for several hours. A foot or more of new snow almost always brings dangerous conditions. The behavior of snow changes with temperature and humidity or with the moisture in the snow. Snow is more dense, for example, when it is warmer — 20° to 30°F (−7° to 0°C). It is lightest and has the most air at colder temperatures, say below 20°F (−7°C). Because of its plastic characteristics, snow actually creeps down a slope. The colder the snow, the less creep or deformation. At warmer temperatures, approximately freezing, snow creeps down a slope fairly quickly, covering several inches or more in an afternoon. In mountainous areas, this phenomenon can sometimes be seen along a roadside, where on a slope that has been undercut by a snowplow, often the top layer of snow will have oozed out over the lower areas below it — an example of snow creep. This tends to settle the snow and stabilize it at warmer temperatures. But if a heavy snowfall comes with cold weather afterward, this process is delayed and the snow may remain unstable for several days.

The pattern of a storm is also important. Snowfall that starts with low temperatures and dry snow but is followed by warmer temperatures and wetter snow is much more likely to cause avalanches. The dry snow at the start of the storm forms a poor bond with the snow below and cannot support the heavier snow deposited later. One of the many interesting aspects of snow concerns its hardness and strength. One pack may be several thousand times stronger than another.

Rapid changes in weather conditions, the wind, temperature, or snowfall cause snowpack adjustments. Be alert to weather changes, for adjustments to snowpack may increase either its stability or the hazard to avalanches.

Wet snowstorms are another general concern. Rain in the spring or warmer winds and cloudy nights associated with late winter can warm the snowcover. The water in the snow can cause wet snow avalanches, which are much more common on south slopes. Wet snow avalanches move much more slowly than a slab avalanche. Many skiers can outrun a wet snow avalanche, whereas a slab avalanche may reach speeds of up to 100 mph. However, wet snow avalanches are dangerous because there is little oxygen in the snow; anyone buried even a short distance under the surface will suffocate.

Several general rules of cross-country travel in snow are worth observing. Before going out, check the local weather forecast. Many western news stations carry warnings of avalanche conditions. If you are near a winter sports area, check with the ski patrol or the snow ranger to determine snow conditions prior to leaving. In the field, look for avalanche paths, since avalanches generally follow the same route over the years. In these areas, trees are swept away, there are often gulleys, and an avalanche is clearly discernible, even after snowfall. The bottom of the slide will often contain rocks, dirt, branches or trees, and other rubble that has been swept down. The surface will obviously be disturbed, even with several inches of fresh snow over it. Look also for recent snow movement. Snowballs or cartwheels of snow that have rolled down a slope are a sign of unstable conditions. The snowpack, even on level ground, may crack or collapse. If snow sounds hollow — an indication that avalanche conditions are present from slabs or depth hoar — the danger is high. Sometimes a skier or the weight of a snow machine will cause cracks to leap through the snow ahead, a serious warning.

Select your route to minimize slide danger. The perfect routes are usually in the valley bottoms, on ridgetops, or on the windward side of a ridge. Be sure to stay away from cornices. It is tempting to ski out onto a cornice, but the snow may be overhung and break off, carrying a skier with it. It is often difficult to locate the true ridgeline in the mountains. A cornice tends to lure a person out on the leeward side of a slope, even though it appears to be the center of a ridge. For that reason, it is better to travel on the windward side, rather than the lee side, of any ridgetop.

It is sometimes difficult to gain a ridgetop without traversing a cornice area. And it is important to avoid disturbing the area below a cornice. In this area snow is often built up heavily in what is called a snow pillow, an area that is susceptible to slab avalanches. Ridgetops must be gained by avoiding and detouring around cornice areas. Never ski or traverse up a slope with a large cornice looming overhead. If you have no other choice but to cross a dangerous slope, it is better to stay near the top or as high as possible. When traveling across a potential avalanche path, those in a group should go one at a time. Let one of the best skiers cross the slope first. Once he reaches the shelter of a grove of trees or an outcropping of rocks, then the next person should go. Several people should not be traversing back and forth across a dangerous slope. It is better to ascend or descend a steep slope as vertically as possible so as to minimize the exposure to an avalanche.

When you are crossing a dangerous slope, there are several things you can do to prepare for an avalanche. First, remove ski pole straps and ski safety straps if you have them. Loosen packs and other equipment. Put on mittens and cap; zip up your coat before crossing an area. Always use an avalanche cord when crossing a hazarous slope. Available from ski shops, the cord is made from bright-colored nylon and is tied to your body. The avalanche cord will ride on top of the snow if you are caught in a slide and allow others in a party quickly to locate you. They find a section of the cord and pull it out of the snow until your body is found. Should you be caught in an avalanche, get away from all equipment and struggle with all possible effort to stay on top or work to the side of the avalanche. If there is ever a time to fight for your life, this is it. The avalanche will tend to tumble and roll a body. Many people are severely injured or even killed by the tumbling action. Just before the snow stops, you must fight for the surface. Get your hands in front of your face and try to make an air space in the snow as the moving pack stops. Try to remain calm. Once you are caught in the snowpack, it is nearly impossible to struggle free unless you are very close to the surface.

When in a group and someone is swept away, be certain to mark the spot where the victim is last seen. Search directly downslope from the last observation. If the victim is not on the surface, quickly search and probe the snow with a stick or ski pole. Look for skis, mittens, or a pack. Those who escaped the avalanche are the victim's hope for survival. Members of the surface party should never desert the area, unless help is only a few minutes away. Survival time of anyone caught in snow rapidly diminishes with time. Those who are not caught in an avalanche should carry ski poles or avalanche poles to search for the victim. If located, he should be treated for suffocation and shock as soon as possible.

Those who do a considerable amount of cross-country skiing in rugged country may want to invest in radio transmitter-receiver systems that are specifically designed for ski and snow-mobile groups. Each member of the party carries a transceiver. Before they leave, the sets are tested and switched to transmit. If any member is buried in an avalanche, the remaining members immediately switch their sets to receive. The buried victim's transmitter can be located by those who survived the avalanche. Some people have estimated that if every person in a party carried a transceiver, survival odds would be raised from an average of 30% to 70%. Always keep in mind that avalanches are very dangerous and that many victims are killed through the mechanical tumbling process which breaks bones and fractures skulls, backs, and necks. Those caught in wet snow avalanches will suffocate in only a few minutes, so while the carrying of a transceiver enhances avalanche safety, it should not be a substitute for prudent methods of travel in the mountains or the study and development of a thorough knowledge of avalanche conditions.

Once you have experienced winter travel in snow, you may have the desire or the opportunity to hike or climb on glaciers. Beautiful and fascinating, glaciers cover only a small part of North America, yet they bring problems and challenges that are unique to mountain travel. For glacier travel, you will need specialized equipment, knowledge, a mastery of climbing techniques, and understanding best gained by travel with experienced people.

Glaciers are created by an excess of winter snow that is deep enough, high enough, or far enough north that it does not entirely melt in the summer months. As the depth of the snow increases, it solidifies into ice and causes a downward flow from its source. Large valley glaciers are essentially rivers of ice, and although ice flow is slow, from a few inches to a few feet each day, it is nevertheless a flow. For the uninitiated, large cracks or riffs called crevasses are the major problem of glaciers. The stresses and strains created by a glacier flowing over irregular terrain create these ice gaps, which may be completely or partially exposed or may have a snow bridge over them. To fall into a crevasse without proper equipment is to perish. Crevasses that look innocent in the warm sunlight can be deep and dangerous. Falling into a crevasse with no assistance is nearly always fatal.

Several features of glaciers must be understood. Most crevasses are on the outside bend of a glacier or in an area where the glacier drops suddenly or the river of ice bends sharply, causing a crack. Even smooth glaciers that are small have a large crevasse at the upper end called a bergschrund. In spring, many inexperienced hikers have climbed up the smooth snow of a small glacier to find themselves stymied at the large foreboding crevasse at the head of the glacier where the weight of the ice has pulled the entire mass away from the rock above.

Even the more innocent terrain around a glacier, such as moraines, can be very hazardous. Moraines are piles of freshly deposited rock, recent in geologic time and very unstable, which have fallen on a glacier and ground out the sides or at the tongue. Moraine rock frequently causes strains, sprained ankles, and broken bones.

Glaciers are among the most interesting and fascinating of mountain phenomena. While this book cannot go into glacial travel in any depth, it should make you aware of the inherent dangers that lie within and beneath the icy beauty of mountain glaciers.

Bears, a source of considerable fear and campfire discussion, are associated with many mountainous parks and wilderness areas. Human fear of bears has grown far out of proportion to the real danger. Learn about bears from a reliable source prior to your trip. Analyze the problem intelligently and take action accordingly. Undoubtedly, bear injuries and fatalities are a very minor part of any wilderness trip. Almost any wilderness hazard is far less dangerous than what we encounter daily in our automobiles and urbanized travel. Indeed, injuries from bears are far fewer than fatalities caused by spiders or bees. Nevertheless, historically bears have been among the few wilderness enemies of man. It is important, therefore, to discern between the two basic species of North American bears.

Black bears are found throughout many roadless and wilderness areas in both eastern and western North America. Relatively docile animals, they are much smaller, far more common than grizzly bears. Normal camp sanitation and avoidance of bears (especially those with cubs) will absolutely minimize any danger from them. Grizzly bears are far different. Unlike black bears, they seldom climb trees, are much larger, much more temperamental, and are distinguished by their humped back and concave face. The grizzly bear is truly the terrible bear written about by Lewis and Clark and many other early explorers. It has been pushed back out of its native plains and valleys to remote mountain parks and wilderness areas. Grizzlies are found primarily in the roadless areas of Idaho, Montana, and Wyoming, as well as in British Columbia, the Yukon and Northwest Territories of Canada, and, of course, Alaska. (Also found in the northern country, primarily in areas of permanent sea ice and the Arctic Ocean, is the polar bear, another species that is dangerous but very seldom encountered.)

Some bear researchers feel that the grizzly bears in the National Parks and wilderness areas have suffered from a type of cultural deterioration. The bears learn that they can obtain food from people, camps, and cabins, and this unnatural behavior, along with aggression toward people, is passed on by the adult females to their young.

Although a close encounter with a grizzly bear is extremely unlikely in a wilderness area, a person who ventures into selected areas of Montana, Idaho, and Wyoming should take precautions, as discussed below. For a grizzly attack, although exceedingly rare, is certainly one of the most ferocious and terrible wilderness encounters that a person can experience.

Bears in wilderness areas have certain natural aggressive tendencies. First and most obvious, females are conditioned to defend their young from other bears and potential enemies. Bears will also defend their food and territory if approached too closely. In addition, some bears that encounter humans show unnatural aggression, actually pursuing people when they are seen from a distance, or chasing horses when there is no obvious explanation for such behavior. A more common problem is extreme boldness expressed by bears when approaching people or campsites. If you encounter a bear with such unnatural tendencies, be extremely cautious, since it has become conditioned to finding food around people and has lost its natural fear of humans. If it is after food, don't protest, but slowly back away. Keep a safe distance from the animal and climb a tree, if possible.

There are several things you can do when entering bear habitat. One is to pack out all garbage and not bury scrap food around the campsite. If you use canned goods, burn the cans or pack them carefully away in plastic sacks so their odor of decaying garbage will not attract any animals. Tie a cord to your food pack and hang it away from the sleeping areas. Be sure to suspend the food high off the gound so a bear cannot reach it. Cook away from sleeping areas, and be sure the sleeping area is not close to a trail or a main route that might be used by bears. Animals often use the same routes that hikers and fishermen use. (Campers in Yellowstone and Glacier parks have been attacked by bears when sleeping on a trail.) If nothing else, having a several-hundred-pound carnivore walk over you in the middle of the night is a terrifying experience. Always keep a clean camp. Clean up dishes and pans immediately after use. Stay alert in bear country and avoid surprising a bear that may be feeding or with young, since it may take immediate agressive action.

Many backpackers travel with several people in a group, so the natural noise and conversation will alert bears prior to their arrival. It is also helpful to have a small bell or other object on a pack that will make noise to alert animals ahead. But don't rely only on noise to discourage bears. Make it a point to learn bear signs. With experience you should easily and clearly distinguish black bear tracks from grizzly bear tracks. The large, dished-out paw print of a grizzly with its claw marks clearly visible is an obvious mark. If bear droppings, signs of bears feeding, or bear tracks are encountered, be especially alert and noisy. Dogs should not be used as protection against bears. (Unleashed dogs are prohibited in many national parks and some wilderness areas.) An untrained or uncontrolled dog may bring an angry bear back toward camp. Finally, learn something about bear behavior and be extremely cautious. If you experience a grizzly bear attack, climb a tree, if you can, for grizzlies cannot climb them easily. If a black bear should attack, climb a tree also. Defense is more successful above a bear in a tree than on the ground.

If you cannot reach a tree quickly, drop a pack or a coat to distract the bear and then move away as unobtrusively and unthreateningly as possible. Sometimes two or three people in a party can shout and wave to keep a bear confused until the initial attack has passed. When a bear is actually upon you, it may be useful to lie on the ground without moving and play dead. There is even one documented case of a person who fainted upon being attacked by a bear and later recovered without serious injury. Of course, as a last resort, if a bear is seriously injuring a person, try to fight it with whatever is available. In Glacier National Park a grizzly once attacked a family of four. The father jumped the grizzly to defend his children. With both arms broken, he drove the bear off with rocks. Such defense against a bear attack is a desperate move. Grizzlies are powerful animals and quick as a cat. It is far better to avoid them.

Keep in mind that the possibility of a grizzly bear attack is remote. In 97 years, grizzlies caused only five deaths in North American national parks. However, people who are attacked by grizzlies usually receive severe disabling injuries. Visitors to grizzly country seldom walk the trails without thinking of the great bear.

One study of grizzly bear attacks in North American parks found that Yellowstone National Park had the highest number of injuries and incidents. Yellowstone was followed by Glacier National Park in Montana, Jasper National Park in Canada, Mt. McKinley National Park in Alaska, Banff and Yoho Parks in Canada. Other parks in Canada and Grand Teton National Park in Wyoming have occasional grizzlies but no record of people being injured.

Most people who were attacked by grizzlies in these parks were hiking in back-country areas or camping in developed campsites. Occasionally bears have attacked those who were provoking them. A study shows that several people were attacked while running away from a grizzly and several were pulled down when they were climbing a tree. There is no doubt that the fastest Olympic sprinter cannot outrun a grizzly bear. It is also obvious that although climbing a tree is the best escape from a grizzly, it must be done very quickly and the person must get 10 or 12 feet (3 – 3.5 meters) off the ground.

Some people have argued that grizzly attacks are so terrible the bear should be eliminated from National Parks and wilderness areas. However, the grizzly has lived in our remote wilderness environments long before the human race crossed the Bering ice bridge and began settlement of North America. The grizzly is normally shy of the human race and has retreated out of its historic environment in valleys and plains to the most remote wilderness areas. The death rate of bear attacks on humans has been only about one person per 30 million visitors in the National Parks — compared to an annual injury rate of over 1.5 million humans hurt in automobile accidents each year or about .7% of the total population of the United States. The risk of a grizzly bear attack is small, but part of the conscious risk a person takes when traveling in grizzly country. Bears enhance a wilderness experience and make the trip, although only mildly dangerous, an invigorating experience. To lose the mystery of bears in a wilderness area is to lose part of the magic that belongs with the wilderness experience.

11

Sea Survival

The wilderness of the sea has long been a challenge. The mystery of currents, winds, ocean storms, and ocean depths has brought both fascination and fear. Nowhere else in the abundant survival literature are there tales to match those of survival at sea. Numerous, often incredible, such stories always have a characteristic of impotence. The fear of ocean vastness, sharks, and other dangers is compounded by the terrible irony of salt water. Death by thirst and by drowning are the two greatest problems. Too little or too much water has always haunted the sailor.

The tales of man's efforts are abundant — Vasco da Gama, Columbus, Magellan, Drake, James Cook, Darwin, Dana, Scott, and Heyerdahl. Few of these men could match the experience of Joshua Slocum and his one-man circumnavigation of the globe near the end of the 19th century. Captain Slocum traveled 26,000 miles on an incredible voyage that lasted four years. At 65, not content to rest on his past achievements, he sailed for Brazil in 1909, and was never seen again.

The risks and dangers of sailing, like those of Slocum and early explorers, are partly reduced with modern radios and equipment. Some of the sea's enigmas are diminished. Every seagoing vessel must carry life jackets and survival gear; for those in cold water areas, survival suits are essential. The modern sailor must realize that he will suffer from hypothermia long before drowning or dying of thirst. As a warm body surrenders its heat to the cold waters, a life jacket is not sufficient. Vital organs are impaired; slowing of the chemical reactions may cause unconsciousness and lead to death. To prolong life in cold water, therefore, fishermen, recreational boaters, and others must have insulative survival clothing — wet suits, special survival suits, or other thermally protective boating garments. They are expensive but, if needed, completely essential.

Water and food should be part of any sea survival gear. Water containers should be strong and collapsible. In addition to fresh water itself, equipment for solar stills and material to collect water should be included. Food can usually be supplemented by fishing. Carry several good-quality fishing lines from 25 lb. to over 100 lb. breaking strength. Stainless steel leaders, various hooks, and several assorted fishing weights will also be needed. Gaff and spearguns may be useful to capture fish near the boat. A fine net can be used to catch plankton, as well as for storing dried fish.

Inflatable rafts, if carried, should contain a complete first-aid kit with any special medicines needed by those aboard. The survival gear should include patches, glue, repair clamps, and stoppers for the raft. In addition, a raft pump in good working condition is essential. Sea anchors, bailers, and spare paddles are indispensable on a raft or small lifeboat.

In addition to the usual survival gear such as a knife, matches, flashlight, and compass, a lifeboat should have signaling equipment: a combination of smoke flares, rocket flares, and modern radio signaling equipment. A mirror or heliograph may also be useful. These items, combined with knowledge of and curiosity about the sea and its life, will greatly enhance survival opportunities.

Boating for an afternoon, a week, or a long cruise is a safe, enjoyable activity. Still, precautions are worthwhile. It is prudent to form a plan of action prior to any possible emergency. Consider the survival priorities and course of action under various weather conditions. If, for example, the weather is fair and problems develop, begin a mental drill. If the boat you are aboard begins to sink, forget about any personal gear or problems. Follow the orders of those who are more experienced and knowledgeable. In cold water wear a survival suit or wool and other warm clothes. Keep a life jacket tightly strapped on. If needed, break out survival gear. Inflate life rafts or help launch lifeboats. Signal for help with standard distress signals such as SOS or Mayday. Be prepared to give the location, the number of the boat, its size and description, as well as details on the number aboard and the nature of the craft's problem. Don't jump overboard in panic. Stay with others aboard and remember that many floundering ships never completely sink. A floundered hull will also be easier for searchers to spot than a small raft or single body in a life jacket.

If you are in a capsizing boat in a storm that requires immediate action by those aboard, be sure to wear a life jacket. A capsizing small boat may throw you into the water without warning. If this should happen, look for the others and the boat. If the boat flips and you are under it, take a gulp of air and dive out from under the boat. Salvage floating cushions and other gear as soon as possible for probable use later.

Once you are in the water, don't strain but rest as much as possible. If other people also are in cold water, huddle together for warmth. Do not swim or thrash around since the motion will only cool your body more rapidly. Don't attempt to swim for shore unless the distance is within easy reach. Stay with the boat, even if it is capsized. Conserve energy whenever possible.

The biggest danger in cold water is death by hypothermia (Chapter 3). The head has a high rate of heat loss due to the inordinate amount of blood in the brain. A wool hat or other cover will help reduce this loss. Keep your head out of the water and remain immobile if possible. The method of drown-proofing often taught in first-aid classes is dangerous in cold water. The technique involves immersing the head in water except for periodic breaths of air above water. This is not advisable in cold water. Research has established a cooling rate while drown-proofing 50% higher than treading water. In cold water, drown-proofing shortens survival time.

Other areas of high heat loss are the neck, the sides of the chest, and the groin area. Protect these areas with insulation, if possible. Survival suits will help a great deal. Put on extra clothing, especially wool if it is available. An outer shell such as a raincoat will also help. Pad the groin area, if possible, to reduce heat loss. Huddling in the water with others significantly lengthens survival time. If you are alone, you can enhance survival by drawing up your knees and wrapping your arms across your chest.

Even relatively warm water can bring on hypothermia. Water temperatures below 68°F (20°C) are dangerous. An unclothed person will be susceptible to hypothermia at that temperature after approximately four hours in the water, or up to eight hours with clothing. (But in an open boat at 68°F he would have few problems.) The hazard of hypothermia increases rapidly as water temperature drops. For example, a drop from 68°F to 57°F (29°C to 15°C) decreases expected survival time from four hours to two hours. A drop from 57°F to 50°F (15°C to 10°C) halves an unclothed person's survival time again, from two hours to one hour. Another 9°F (5°C) drop in water temperature cuts survival time to 30 minutes or less. At such cold temperatures, a person attempting to swim a mere 100 yards may become disabled and lose consciousness.

Thermally-protective clothing greatly increases survival times in cold water. For example, in 50°F (10°C) water, swimming survival time is only one hour. Staying immobile increases survival to nearly three hours. A good thermal suit will raise survival time to ten hours or more under the same conditions. But even clothing such as wool will often double survival time.

Thirst, the age-old problem of men at sea, has driven sailors to desperate solutions. During World War II, a shipwrecked naval lieutenant was floating on a small rubber raft in the Pacific. Thirsty and frustrated, he watched a sea bird land on the ocean and drink its fill of water. Angry that the bird could drink water while he couldn't, the lieutenant shot the bird. He then cut open the bird and traced its digestive system. Around the intestines he found abundant fat, and with his deranged logic he decided that if he greased his mouth with the fat, he could swallow sea water. It was a bizarre, desperate conclusion. He began to drink small amounts in this way for several days. His story was widely publicized and given as a survival tip to other military personnel. However, it was a dangerous, erroneous conclusion — later disproved by medical personnel. The naval officer had survived not because of the sea water, but despite it. What saved his life was rainwater he had gathered from a storm. Physiological research has shown that drinking sea water shortens rather than prolongs survival time.

Thirst and dehydration — in the desert as well as on the sea — follow the same pattern. With increasing deficiencies in water, thirst and discomfort begin in the body's painful dehydration march, then lassitude, loss of appetite, sleepiness, and a rise in body temperature. Dehydration of 5% body weight causes nausea. At 6% to 10% dehydration, the victim will have headaches, dizziness, tingling in the extremities, and an inability to walk. Water loss in excess of 10% often brings delirium, and some senses begin to fail, especially hearing, but sometimes vision, as the body loses its vital fluid. Fatal dehydration depends on the air temperature and the rate of dehydration, but a 25% loss of body weight is fatal at any temperature. At 90°F (32°C), 15% dehydration is fatal. In desert regions, death from dehydration is often accelerated by high temperatures and low humidity. But a delirious mind and the ever-present torment of sea water bring premature death to many shipwrecked sailors.

An age-old curse, the inability to drink sea water, remains a source of myths, some of which are dangerous. At the turn of the century, a shipwrecked scientist gave sea water enemas to his companions. His report that the sailors survived and flourished gained widespread attention. He claimed that intestinal walls unlike the stomach walls, filtered out harmful salts. Later disproven by researchers, the myth of sea water enemas survived into the World War II era.

Some believe that few shipwreck survivors die of dehydration alone. A British study on sea survival, for example, concluded that as dehydration increases to about 15% of body weight, the will to resist drinking sea water decreases. Finally, the victim succumbs and drinks sea water. Death results. The author of a British study on thirst, MacDonald Critchley, provides this description of a dehydrated person who drinks sea water. There is

> immediate slaking, followed quite soon by an exacerbation of the thirst, which will require still more copious draughts. The victim then becomes silent and apathetic . . . with a peculiar fixed and glassy expression in the eyes. The condition of the lips, mouth and tongue worsens, and a peculiarly offensive odor has been described in the breath. Within an hour or two, delirium sets in, quiet at first but later violent and unrestrained; consciousness is gradually lost. The color of the face changes and froth appears at the corners of the lips. Death may take place quietly . . . more often it is a noisy termination . . .

Not a pleasant description, yet it is the result of drinking sea water when dehydrated. Nevertheless, careful dilution of sea water has been successfully tried. Thor Heyerdahl sailed the raft *Kon-Tiki* across the Pacific in 1947 to establish the point that aborigines could have done the same. On the three-month journey, he and his men regularly added 20% to 40% salt water to their freshwater supplies with no ill effects.

Modern desaltation kits provide a method of converting salt water to fresh. A solar still, used aboard ship to distill fresh water from sea water, can produce about two pints of water per day. Carrying emergency water, desalting kits, and solar stills is superior to drinking sea water. Sea water is as undrinkable today as it was for Coleridge's Ancient Mariner.

Hunger has always been a great problem at sea. In 1521, on the pioneering voyage across the Pacific, Magellan and his crew went three months without fresh fruit and vegetables. One of his crew wrote

> We ate biscuits which were no longer biscuits, but powder of biscuits swarming with worms, for they had eaten the food. It stank strongly of the urine of rats. We ate ox hides that covered the top of the mainyard . . . Rats were sold for one-half ducat apiece, and even then we could not get them.

While the sea has abundant life and food in many areas, the problem of capturing and preparing it can be more difficult than on land. Nevertheless, with adequate gear and preparation, sea food is usually available.

Many foods, especially protein, consume water in the digestive process and are not craved aboard ship when thirst is a problem. Nevertheless, wet protein, as found in freshly caught fish or turtle, counteracts the fluid loss to a certain extent. Additionally, food intake, while not as essential as water, is beneficial in maintaining strength and the ability to work.

A person lost on a raft or boat has little chance to pick and choose his food. Much like a hunting savage, he must adjust to primal eating practices. But most important, a castaway must try to remain coherent and strong. To do this, he must consume some food and, if possible, must capture and store extra food, such as fish. People have lived for long periods on life rafts. Aboard the S.S. *Ben Lomond* when it was torpedoed in 1942, Poon Kim, a Hong Kong native, subsisted on rainwater, fish, and survival rations, until he was picked up in good condition 173 days later.

Poon Kim and other castaways have found all fish, including scavengers, are good to eat. However, fish liver must be eaten in moderation; otherwise you may become ill from excessive vitamins. Lobsters, crabs, crayfish, and other shellfish found in shallow waters or along shores are edible.

Some sea birds, while difficult to catch, provide a good source of nutrition. So do bird bones and the marrow of turtles. Fat from birds and sea creatures is useful as a lotion for protection from the sun and salt water. Often, sea birds can be caught with a baited hook and line. Just wait for a bird to swallow a floating bait, then pull it in.

Far from land, birds might be difficult to locate, but fishing is always possible. Line fishing is often the most practical method of catching fish. Use strong tackle. Try hooks, baits, and various depths of water. Experiment with aluminum from survival kits or flashy spoons for bait. Capture small fish close to the boat with a net or trap and use them for bait later. Trial and error is the best method to learn fishing skills anywhere at any time. But in some regions, it is possible to hook a shark or other large fish with an unfortunate loss of gear. Don't be too ambitious.

Small bait dropped overboard or a light at night may attract fish, which may then be captured by using a gaff or spear. Don't risk losing the gaff or spear by attempting too large a prey. Although a spear may be improvised from a knife, take care that the knife is not lost.

Small nets can be trailed behind a raft or boat to capture small bait fish or plankton. A bail bucket or other container can also be improvised into a fish trap with a little effort. As is the case in any survival emergency, plastic, cord, wire, or any containers have many potential uses.

Once they are brought aboard, most smaller fish can be killed with a sharp blow to the back of the head. A stout club made from flotsam or the blunt side of a knife will usually dispatch a modest-sized fish. Take care with the types of reef fish that have spiky dorsal fins and venomous stings. Kill larger fish by breaking their necks or cutting off their heads. Paralyze smaller fish by pressing firmly on their eyes with your thumb and index finger.

The flesh of most species of marine life can be sun dried. Cut fish, turtle flesh, and other sea creatures into strips an inch thick for air drying. Thinner strips will dry quicker. Hang such strips of flesh on lines and turn them occasionally to aid in the drying process.

Fishing for food may bring a castaway into contact with sharks, among the most feared creatures of the sea. Sharks exist in all the oceans. Primitive and unfeeling, the shark symbolizes a diabolical creature. Yet of the more than 325 species of sharks, only a score or so are known to attack humans. Of these, the most dangerous are the great whites, tiger, maho, hammerhead, and sand sharks. Cruising sharks, those whose fins project above the water line, forage in shallow water and even ascend rivers. Because of their feeding habits in shallow water, these species are often in contact with humans.

Temperate water sharks are the least aggressive, while those from tropical and subtropical waters are the most aggressive. All sharks are voracious feeders and may travel either in packs or singly. Cruising sharks investigate floating objects, and because they have well-developed senses of smell, they are attracted to blood. They are also sensitive to vibrations sent through the water by injured or dying prey. A poorly coordinated swimmer may also attract attention. Although most shark attacks are directed toward people who are floating or swimming, people in small boats or rafts have also been attacked. As late as the start of World War II, shark attacks were considered a minor risk of sea survival. As the war progressed, however, thousands of sailors and soldiers witnessed or survived shark attacks. When the U.S.S. *Juneau* was torpedoed in 1942, most of the crew was killed immediately, but 150 men were thrown into the water. After the weakest had drowned, the sharks began to finish off the wounded. For days, the shrinking number of survivors fought the sharks and the urge to give up. Only ten survived. Research was conducted and survivors of the *Juneau* and other sinking ships were systematically interviewed. Several guidelines emerged on how to repel sharks.

Naval researchers concluded that swimmers should retain all their clothing, especially their shoes. Those without clothing were often attacked first. Others suffered from abrasions caused when the rough skin of sharks scraped against them. Swimming movements should always be free and easy to minimize attracting a cruising shark. Erratic movement signals to a shark that a victim is disabled and unable to defend himself.

It was also established that people should stay together in the water. Several people can ward off an attack easier than a lone swimmer. If an attack actually starts, kick and thrash at the shark. If possible, hit it in the eyes or gills, or on the nose. Shouting sometimes helps. In a raft or boat, however, it is better to keep quiet and not attract attention. Keep hands, legs, feet, and equipment inside the raft. If possible, don't jettison blood, vomit, or refuse; the garbage will attract sharks. If a shark passes a raft too closely, it may abrade the flotation chambers and cause leaks. Thus, a passing shark should be driven off with an oar or paddle. Scaring off a passing shark is important because if it does attack, it will often bring others. Voracious feeders and cannibalistic, sharks even attack and devour their own injured brothers and sisters.

Jellyfish, especially the Portuguese man-of-war, can cause painful, even crippling stings. Barracuda and other scavenger fish may attack survivors if they are not vigorously repelled. Killer whales have also reportedly attacked some small craft.

If a castaway successfully copes with cold water, hunger, dehydration, and sharks, the next concern is usually navigation. In the absence of navigational equipment, a survival craft can only use rough estimates of travel. With modern equipment, however, arrival time at a destination and the best direction of travel can be determined with considerable accuracy. This can be important in determining the rationing of food and water, as well as the possibility of securing additional supplies by rainfall, bird migrations, and passing busy sea lanes.

Without instruments, navigation is essentially a system of estimating the effect of wind and current on a raft. Sea lanes, possible rainwater, and dominant winds and currents are essential items to consider in selecting a route. Much of this information is on ocean charts or maps carried in life rafts. Wind and current will dictate the route. A raft with no paddles can travel 40 miles a day down current or downwind. Yet, a party may exhaust themselves paddling against a current and make no progress whatsoever.

When crossing shipping lanes, lookouts should be posted. Signaling devices should be readily available, but even some modern ships on automatic pilot may not have anyone on deck. Even close at hand, a raft may pass these ships unseen. Don't exhaust the supply of flares and signals or despair at failure to flag down the first passing ship.

Understanding weather is another important aspect of navigation. Forecasting weather is helpful in preparing for storms, rainfall, or other kinds of situations. At sea, a successful forecaster reads cloud processes and relates them to changes in wind and ocean swell patterns. As with other natural phenomena, a healthy curiosity and the questioning of experienced seamen help develop skills in weather forecasting, which, in turn, leads to more accurate forecasts. Storms and elementary weather forecasting are discussed in Chapter 8.

Once a survival craft approaches land, several changes are noticeable. One of the first signs of land is the increase in the number and variety of birds. Isolated sightings are undependable indicators, since the avians may be migrating or be carried far to sea by storms. But an abundance of birds is a dependable indicator. Another signal of land is the changing, lighter color of the sea as the continental shelf rises to meet the craft. The sea sometimes takes on a light green tinge.

As one approaches land, one of the first signs after visual sighting is the sound of breakers. Tropical coasts often smell of vegetation that is carried many miles out to sea. Lights from coastal cities may be visible in the night sky for 100 miles (60 km.) under ideal conditions. High mountains may be seen for 50 miles (30 km.) in clear weather, but may still require three or four days to reach, especially if offshore winds are strong at night. Under some atmospheric conditions, sea-level objects may be sighted 40 miles (24 km.) ahead with astonishing clarity. Such abnormal refractions are a type of mirage caused by warm air above the cold water surface. Even though coastal objects may appear nearby, don't squander distress flares until you are actually close to land.

Landing on shore may be one of the most difficult feats that you face. Dehydrated and weakened, you may not be able to stand or walk. Therefore, if at all possible, don't try to land in a surf. If possible, never arrive directly on a shore that faces the sea, because rocks and undertows will be dangerous there. Although headlands are the worst areas in which to land a boat, the opposite side of a headland is ideal. Any beach where the surf bends around a point of land is safer than areas that receive the direct frontal assault of waves.

When a landing is imminent, tie down food and water to prevent its loss. A light sea anchor may help stabilize the raft if you are landing in surf. Wear a life jacket and clothing for protection from rocks and surf. Floating objects such as crates and life jackets can help you ride the surf to the shore. If your life raft flips, take care to avoid being trapped under it. In a rigid boat, avoid oars and heavy equipment as well as the boat itself if it turns. Be prepared to jump clear. The surf may smash down on you and do considerable bodily injury. Upon reaching shore, salvage the boat or raft and the other equipment, if the beach is isolated, because such items may be useful. In the case of cold water immersion, you may need to make a fire or find warm shelter to prevent hypothermia.

After any sea survival experience, even after reaching land, be conservative with supplies and equipment. On an island or isolated beach, a land survival experience may be in store. Daniel Defoe's classic novel *Robinson Crusoe*, depicting a survival epic on an ocean island, was based on the adventures of Alexander Selkirk, a Scottish sailor, who lived alone for over four years after he was marooned on the Juan Fernandez Islands early in the 18th century. Many coasts and islands are isolated even today. After survival at sea, take every precaution until survival on land is assured.

12

Preparation

Early explorers sought out experienced travelers from whom to learn survival skills. Captain Robert Falcon Scott, prior to his ill-fated polar expedition, visited Norway's Fridtjof Nansen, a veteran arctic explorer. Nansen's advice was that Scott use dogs for hauling supplies. When food ran low, the same animals would provide food. Scott, however, declined to use dogs. Although he and four companions reached the South Pole, on the way back they all died of hunger and cold, only a few miles from abundant supplies, knowing that Roald Amundsen had reached the pole a month before them. Amundsen had returned safely after successfully using dogs first for transportation and, when needed, for food.

The Donner Party, a group of Midwestern farmers bound for California in 1846, was guided by Lansford Hastings, who convinced the group that he had pioneered a "shortcut" across the Salt Lake desert to the Sierra Nevada. "Hastings cutoff" became a notorious disaster that left the wagon train stranded in the High Sierra at the start of an unusually severe winter. The famous survival epic ended with starvation and cannibalism — and a lesson on the choice of guides.

Today's wilderness traveler, on land or sea, still needs experienced advice and assistance, yet even today advice from others should be tempered with caution and individual preferences. Most people will begin learning about nature, backpacking, and survival from experienced friends or in a classroom. Others will learn from those they meet along the trail. Local chapters of conservation, hiking, or outdoor clubs are excellent sources of experience and information. Yet it should always be remembered that sometimes even formal leaders on organized outdoor trips may be unprepared for a new environment. There is no substitute for personal knowledge of the natural world, intelligent curiosity and experience, occasionally painfully earned.

An inexperienced hiker who has the opportunity to join a hike or climb with strangers should not be bashful about questioning their experience and background. A sharp look at equipment and clothing will give some indication of the group's competence. A few years ago, a group of Grand Teton National Park rangers gathered for the nighttime recovery of a body, the victim of a 300-foot fall. A young man had fallen to his death in a steep, remote canyon, and although the recovery was important, it was not urgent. The leader of the rescue party failed to check the equipment of one husky ranger. Later that night, it was discovered the man was wearing cowboy boots on his first mountain rescue. He was useless on the steep, rocky slopes and a danger to himself and others as the slick soles and poor ankle support of the boots hampered his travel. As any experienced hiker knows, cowboy boots are made for riding horses or bar stools, not for hikes or rugged country.

In any group, it is important to consider the health and physical fitness of individuals. If medical problems exist, a doctor should provide appropriate medication and certify the person for the trip. More important than physical condition is the mental attitude of the individuals in a group. Temperamental, moody, or fearful people, or those indifferent and forgetful of the rest, may cause problems on an extended trip. Among experienced friends, individual differences usually are not important. Social life does not disappear at the boundary of a wilderness area. The enjoyment and safety of any group may depend upon social considerations, as well as on equipment and physical condition.

Before starting, every person in a group should understand the length and difficulty of the trip that is planned. Essential survival kits and first-aid equipment should be available to all. Details of food, stoves, tents, and other community gear should be discussed. Duplication should be avoided, but essential gear should not be left behind. Some agreement should be reached on the group pace, the distance to be traveled, and the route. For those who may have difficulty, alternate plans should be developed, and no peer pressure should be exerted to force a person into country or terrain he is uncomfortable with. Potential hazards such as animals or weather should be considered, and techniques for coping with them should be understood by everyone.

Physical preparation for any wilderness journey is useful. In many cases, the difference between an enjoyable, pleasant trip and a strenuous, hazardous one is the amount of physical preparation. Conditioning of the heart and lungs through running and other activities is beneficial. The longer the wilderness trip or the more difficult the mountaineering expedition or sailing trip, the better condition a person should be in.

Everyone has the ability to adapt physically and mentally. The human body adjusts to a certain extent to heat, cold, high altitudes, and different barometric pressures. But it is also important to remember that the range of individual adaptation varies widely. Some individuals, physically fit and otherwise healthy, cannot adapt to high elevation. Others adjust readily to such conditions and avoid the common problem of mountain sickness. Physical conditioning and proper nutrition are essential for everyone. Preparation for heat and cold is possible. Most important, however, is the mental conditioning for a strenuous journey.

Emotional functions have a substantial impact on survival ability and attitude. The exact mechanism is not understood by scientists but is often appreciated by those in a wilderness experience. The physiological indications of what has been termed the human defense reaction are profound. A host of muscular, cardiovascular, and other impacts can be measured. In a crisis, reflexes automatically override the higher levels of the brain. Adrenalin and other chemicals create the ability to do extraordinary feats. Everyone carries the wilderness heritage to perform incredible actions in a crisis.

A hiker in a Western national park suddenly encountered a cow moose with a young calf a few yards ahead on the trail. One look at the charging moose, hackles up, ears back, nose flared, hoofs slashing, triggered an immediate and strong defensive reaction in the hiker. Without thinking, he leaped into a nearby tree and found himself on a branch well out of reach of the moose, his pulse pounding in his ears, muscles shaking, breath short and fast. When he calmed down, the hiker was stunned to find that his heavy pack, with sleeping bag, food, tent, and other gear was still on his back. Later, when the moose ushered her calf into the woods, he climbed out of the tree. He then discovered that even without his pack he could not jump and reach the lowest branch of the tree. Yet at the moment the moose charged, he had done just that with a loaded pack on his back. He never completely remembered how he got to the branch.

The hiker's reaction was part of an ancient survival mechanism of the human race. He did not think; he only reacted. A person does little to prepare for such a reaction. It lies dormant, but it is important to know of its existence and to realize that the human body is capable of extraordinary feats under emergency conditions. In an evolutionary sense, man is both adaptable and a fierce, tough predator. The hereditary remnants are always there in the most urbanized modern world.

Instinct will not help in the choice of equipment. The gear a person buys should be carefully selected. The equipment in a boat, camper, or pack is the link between civilization and the roadless environment. Product quality varies greatly and, unfortunately, the rise of camping and hiking as popular outdoor activities has brought a great deal of inferior equipment onto the market. Failure of gear can produce discomfort and inconvenience at best and downright danger under some conditions. Finally, the cost of outdoor products requires that gear be carefully chosen and the choice be a wise one. Fortunately, most major items such as packs, sleeping bags, and tents are generally durable and long lasting.

Personal needs are the most important consideration in selecting gear. For the beginner, the choice of equipment is confusing. Only time and experience will create the definite preferences that most outdoor people affect. It is important not to rush out and buy all the equipment initially. Many mountain shops rent equipment at reasonable rates. Universities and colleges have recreation clubs that rent camping equipment. The beginner has a chance to try out various types of equipment and to develop unique preferences. Observe what other experienced people are using; ask why they like it. Shop around and compare different brands of sleeping bags and packs. Some of the hiking and camping magazines have excellent equipment evaluations; check the back issues. Advertisements are also useful in comparing the claims and details of various outdoor items. Generally, mountaineering and skiing specialty shops have the best equipment available. Several companies have outstanding equipment catalogs that provide countless hours of enjoyable daydreaming. Department stores, with a few exceptions, generally have the poorest-quality materials and equipment.

Quality and price are usually closely related. However, watch out for fads. A cheap sleeping bag, tent, or pair of boots usually will last only a short time. Good quality costs money, but for the serious hiker or camper, quality is worth the extra money. Always look for items that will serve more than one use. The roadside camper who needs a sleeping bag can just as easily spend a little more and get a high-quality lightweight bag, which will serve roadside camping yet be useful if he takes up backpacking. A heavyweight bulky tent for use in a campground is useless for backpacking. A lightweight durable backpack tent will cost more but will last a long time. It can be used for all types of camping and has the advantage of being compact, an important consideration with the trend toward smaller cars.

Good boots are the foundation of any outdoor person's gear. Boots are expensive and must be selected with care. First consider the type of boot needed. Some ambitious rock climbers buy a specialized climbing boot or kletter shoe at first. For the novice, such a lightweight climbing shoe, specialized and limited in its possible use, provides little ankle support and is a waste of money. The thin soles are designed for gripping rock. Advanced climbers need such specialized shoes, but not the beginning hiker or backpacker.

Trail shoes are often available at a reasonable price and usually are a good first boot. More a shoe than a boot, they are designed for trails where footing is usually secure. Because they are lightweight, they require little breaking in. They are popular for casual wear, as well as for lightweight trail use. One pound of weight on the foot is equivalent to five pounds on the back; therefore, such lightweight shoes are practical.

Hiking boots are stiffer and heavier than trail shoes and suitable for rougher terrain. They are designed to provide more ankle and foot support. Unlike trail shoes, they need to be broken in. Because they are well made and provide good protection in many conditions, they are the best all-around outdoor boot.

Mountaineering boots are heavy and extremely stiff. Like climbing shoes, they are specialized and should be purchased for mountaineering expeditions. Useful on ice, rock, and snow, they provide excessive protection for general use; they are also expensive and difficult to break in. Nevertheless, some hikers who want one good pair of boots mistakenly purchase heavy mountaineering boots. This is pedestrian overkill and should be resisted. Mountaineering boots are not the only specialized boots available. Insulated pacs or waterproof boots are popular with snowmobilers. They are bulky and warm but are not designed for hiking or walking.

Boots are also classified according to sole construction and the method by which soles are fastened to the upper boots. The first method, termed a cemented weld, involves gluing an inexpensive type of sole to the upper boot. There is no midsole or stitching or enough support in such boots. To identify cemented weld boots, look for the absence of stitching and the lack of a midsole or middle layer between the inner sole and lug sole.

Injection molding is a fairly recent method of boot construction. Molten neoprene is applied under pressure to attach the upper boot to the sole. The injected welt replaces glue or stitching. Boots with injection molding are usually relatively inexpensive and are impossible to resole. Trail shoes are commonly found with injection molding.

A better method of boot construction has outside stitching and employs a welt. There are several types of welt boot construction of varying degrees of quality. Such welts have one, two, or even three rows of stitching. Replacing soles on such boots is fairly easy. Depending on the type of stitching, the boots can be waterproofed, are flexible and of generally good quality. Virtually all quality hiking and mountaineering boots utilize a welt system sole. A few years ago, an outer sole with high carbon neoprene and a lug pattern was considered the only fine hiking sole available. Today there are several types for various hiker preferences, including those that minimize trail damage and erosion.

The upper boot quality often depends on the leather used. Cowhide is split into thin sheets suitable for boot tops. The outside layer is smooth and termed "top grain." It is flexible, tough, and naturally resistant to moisture. Such leather is superior for boot construction. Less expensive boots have "split" leather that is rough, difficult to waterproof, and subject to stretching. Seams in the upper boot are difficult to waterproof. In selecting a boot, the one with the fewest seams is usually the best and most expensive. The ideal hiking boot will be constructed of one piece of leather with a single seam on the outside of the boot. Depending on the quality of boots, they will be lined and have "shanks" or support arches built in. They may have foam padding and a roll of padding around the top to keep out pebbles.

Proper boot fit is essential. Although quality hiking boots are available from mail order houses, experienced assistance may be needed to secure a quality fit. The standard procedure to determine a good fit is to wear hiking socks to try the boots on. Put the boot on but do not lace it. Slide the foot forward as far as it will go. While you are standing straight, someone should be able to slide his index finger behind the heel to the boot sole. If he can get two fingers to the sole, the shoe is too loose. If he can't get a finger completely to the sole, the fit is too tight. Then try some knee bends. The heel should slide up in the boot only slightly, no more than an eighth of an inch or so. Try on several pairs of boots and walk around the showroom. Take time to find a comfortable fit.

Clothing is a minor concern to most hikers, backpackers, and outdoor types. Fortunately, fashionable clothing has not afflicted most outdoor activities, except downhill skiing and some pleasure sailing circles. Old work clothes, military surplus gear, almost anything warm and comfortable, is adequate.

The important thing to consider in clothing is a layer system. Layers of clothes are warmer and provide flexibility under a variety of conditions. It is useful to have three layers available. The ventilating layer next to the skin should have an open weave. Wearing fishnet-type underwear helps one avoid the clammy sensation when wet with sweat. Cotton T-shirts are practical and don't chafe as do synthetic fibers or wool.

The next layer is an insulating layer. It might be a wool shirt or sweater or vest. The insulating layer, especially if it contains goose down, should be kept dry. Wool is preferred since it retains its warmth while damp, one of the few materials with this feature. Down is excellent, but it has virtually no insulating properties when wet. Some of the synthetic materials combine the best features of wool and down.

The outer, protective layer should be windproof or waterproof. Most people prefer zippers or buttons on both the insulating and protective layers. Zippers provide a range of protection that pullover clothing lacks. A hooded windbreaker is also important because of the high portion of heat that is lost from the head and through the neck by convection. Most parkas are not completely waterproof, since the material must "breathe" to permit body moisture to escape. Although some synthetic fabrics are breathable and waterproof, they are expensive and involve special care and handling. For this reason, boaters and hikers in heavy rainfall areas prefer separate rain gear.

Depending on the conditions that are expected, a variety of raincoats, rain parkas, or rainsuits will be needed. Some hikers prefer ponchos that double as emergency shelters or ground cloths.

Personal preferences and finances will determine what is suitable. The only items that are unacceptable, except for an emergency, are plastic rain gear. They tear and snag and seldom last more than a few days or even hours in some conditions. Heavier, coated nylon and other fabrics are far superior and well worth the extra expense.

Extra socks are useful on extended trips. The most serviceable varieties are wool blends that are reinforced for added strength. Some special hiking socks are good but expensive. Many prefer a thin nylon sock inside a wool pair for comfort and to prevent blisters. Discover your personal preferences by wearing boots around the house prior to a trip. Keep extra pairs of socks on hand so your feet will be dry and comfortable.

Depending on the weather, you should carry hats and mittens. On warm sunny trips, a loose straw hat is comfortable. Visor hats protect the eyes, but do nothing to shelter the head from sunlight. A wool stocking cap is an old standby for cold weather. Climbers and cavers require hardhats for safety. Most individuals will choose a hat that reflects their personality and sense of comfort.

Sleeping bags may be filled with goose down, duck down, feathers, or a synthetic fiber, usually a variety of polyester or polyurethane. Traditionally, the finest and lightest-weight bags were filled with goose down. Cheaper "down" bags usually have feathers or duck down, inferior insulating materials. In recent years, synthetic fillers have improved in quality. They are waterproof and are considerably cheaper than goose down. For children's bags or sleeping bags that will be used under wet conditions, such as on a boat, synthetic fillers have distinct advantages. As in the case of boots, careful shopping for sleeping bags is needed. Compare price, quality, and opinions of experienced owners of various bags. Unlike boots, some of the best sleeping bags are available through mail order outdoor supply outlets.

Most backpackers prefer a three-season bag with approximately 2 pounds (1 kg.) of down filler. Such a bag is adequate except under very cold or winter conditions. For winter or mountaineering conditions you will require a heavier bag. Ideally, a sleeping bag should have a full-length zipper. Bags with such zippers provide more ventilation on warm nights, can be paired with similar bags for couples, and can be unzipped and used as a quilt.

Baffles are the internal walls of a sleeping bag that hold the filler in place. Several types of baffles influence the price, quality, and warmth of sleeping bags. Beware of baffles with sewn-through construction; bags with such baffles look like quilts, with stitching completely through each seam. Except on the warmest nights, these bags are cold because they lack insulation at the seams. The only desirable feature of sewn-through is the cost, as it's the cheapest form of construction. Laminated baffles are a double row of walls that create a warm but bulky sleeping bag cover. They are expensive. Many bags have a box or slant wall system of baffles that are warm but not bulky.

Another item to consider in a bag is its loft — the height of a bag after it is flattened out. Compare loft of various bags on the floor of the salesroom. The higher the loft, the warmer the bag. Body weight crushes the bottom loft of a bag and greatly reduces insulation. The crushed loft is the reason a foam pad or other insulation is needed under a sleeping bag for both comfort and warmth.

The shells or outer coverings of most bags are rip-stop nylon. Such coverings are lightweight, abrasion resistant, yet permit the bag to breathe. A sleeping bag must not be waterproof; a pint or more of body moisture must escape the shell during a night's sleep. To test this, wrap a sleeping bag in a plastic shell and climb in. Soon your body will have a clammy feeling as the moisture accumulates in the bag. By morning, the bag will be wet and you will be cold.

Sleeping bags come in several shapes, from mummy bag to roomy rectangular bedrolls. Mummy bags are the lightest and warmest, but some people have difficulty adjusting to the form-fitting interior. Rectangular bags are heaviest and not suitable for backpacking. Many popular bags are a compromise between mummy bags and roomy rectangular bags. Most good bags have a hood attached with a drawstring. On cold nights the cord is pulled around the head for additional warmth.

Check the quality of stitching in sleeping bags. Look for uniform stitches and at least ten stitches per inch. Corners and areas of stress should be reinforced. Invite an experienced seamstress along for advice on comparing the quality of workmanship. A quality bag will look good to the experienced eye. Shoddy workmanship is hard to hide.

Once you purchase a sleeping bag, it is important to take good care of it. Down insulation is made largely of protein and lanolin, tough natural products. Be sure to keep the bag dry; some backpackers lightly dry their bag in a machine dryer after each trip. Direct sunlight can damage the oils in the down and deteriorate the nylon outer shell. Sunlight is the one element that will affect nylon, which is not seriously harmed by moisture and mildew.

Store a down bag carefully. Don't leave the bag stuffed in a sack or tightly compressed. It is better to leave it loose or folded on a shelf. Wash it gently in a bathtub, not in an automatic washer, and use a mild soap or a down soap found in many specialty catalogs and stores for backpackers. Don't lift the bag out of the water without squeezing out the moisture; otherwise the internal walls, or baffles, which hold the down in place, may burst under the weight of the water. After a couple of good rinses, dry the bag by rolling it several times in dry towels. When the bulk of the moisture is out, dry the bag in a machine dryer carefully. Check it often to make sure it doesn't get too hot. Synthetic materials are easier to care for than down.

If you are camped and discover that your bag is not warm enough for the conditions, there are several things you can do. First, a tent or shelter will be 5°–10°F (3°–6°C) warmer than the outside temperature. A shelter will also cut down on the wind chill. You can gain additional warmth by placing two sleeping bags together. The body warmth of two or three people huddled together will effectively raise the temperature, especially in a tent. Remember to camp up a slope and away from streams and lakes to be in warmer conditions. Finally, as needed, put on extra clothes, sweaters, and other items for maximum warmth. Don't overdo it; for if you begin to sweat, the end result may be uncomfortable chilling.

A tent is the home or shelter to carry in a pack, boat, or vehicle. Before purchasing a tent, decide on the most common conditions for using the tent and the appropriate size. If you are traveling to rainy areas, get a roomy tent, because you will need to store gear in it. If you will be camping and traveling where there is substantial humidity, remember to find a tent with plenty of ventilation so condensation will not be a serious problem. For areas such as the North Woods, with abundant insects and mosquitoes, be sure to find a tent that has good netting and protection from such critters. Alpine conditions require a tent that will withstand heavy winds. Before even a modest gale, many otherwise suitable tents will collapse into a twisted mess of aluminum poles and line. Desert conditions demand a tent that is well ventilated but able to withstand periodic heavy winds. If in doubt, rent a tent for a trip or seek the advice of an experienced tent camper.

One of the first things to consider is the weight of a tent. Extremely lightweight tents or sleeping bag shelters are available, and under some conditions they may be adequate. They can also be carried for emergencies. Most good lightweight tents are made of nylon or a combination of synthetic materials. For the combination of weight and strength, they are usually the best. Canvas or cotton tents are heavy, subject to mildew and rot.

A well-made tent has straight seams and looks good when set up. A good tent is tight and smooth, but a loose, flapping tent is noisy and may tear in a substantial wind. Because a completely waterproof tent cannot breathe, most tents have a waterproof fly. Such a fly may be left behind for a desert trip, but it will be essential on a mountain trip. It should cover a tent generously and have top-quality workmanship.

A cotton tent should not be stored unless it is clean and dry. Nylon tents need not be completely dry but they are especially vulnerable to intense sunlight and heat. Always be careful when you use campfires; sparks may blow onto a nylon tent and burn holes in the fabric. Never fill a gas stove in a tent; nylon burns and melts easily. A stove carelessly kicked over inside a tent can be a disaster for the tent, the sleeping bags, and the occupants.

Many tents have elaborate, sophisticated designs for various purposes. The oldest design for mountain use is the A-frame tent. Most mountain tents have been of this type, partly because of the simple design and partly because they can withstand windstorms. Since the days of the pioneer mountaineer Edward Whymper, the A-frame has been a classic. Another dependable old design is a large one-pole tent, which is usually designed for three or four people. A tall single pole holds up the center. A more modern design is a dome or semidome tent, which is lightweight for the surface it covers and usually withstands wind quite well. Such a tent is held in place by an elaborate set of wands or poles. A modification of this type of tent is the exoskeleton tent, with poles holding up the tent from the outside. This tent is self-supporting and once erected may be carried to another spot without being dismantled. Some tents with this design collapse in high winds, however. In all cases, look for a design that suits the conditions you expect to encounter, but also consider a tent that is simple and easy to erect.

Packs are a special item for backpackers. As with other equipment, the choice of a pack must depend on its anticipated use. A day pack may be used for short trips, bicycling, or trips to the library. A rucksack may be used for a longer trip, a cross-country ski trip that requires more survival gear, or a summit climb. A frame pack is used for longer trips and comes in a variety of types and shapes. Consider the quality carefully and shop around. Backpacking magazines have conducted evaluations of packs which aid immensely in the decision-making process.

On a boat, in a motor vehicle, or for backpacking, a stove is becoming an essential item. Regulations for many wilderness areas now prohibit campfires because of their impact on the environment and the shortage of wood. Several lightweight stoves are available. An older type, often the heaviest available, is a kerosene stove. Although it is bulky, some people prefer it because of the availability of fuel almost anywhere in the world. Kerosene is also slightly less explosive than gasoline. Some lightweight stoves have disposable propane or butane cartridges, which are light, convenient, and usually efficient but are also wasteful and costly. The supply of cartridges is also a problem in some areas. The most popular stoves use white gas, but a few will burn on automobile gasoline; a wide variety is available. Consider the quality and weight of the stove; some of the lightest stoves are rather fragile. If you anticipate rough or extended use, get a heavier but more durable stove.

Knives are a constant source of discussion and argument among serious outdoor people. The type of knife you select should depend upon the anticipated use. But personality often enters into the decision. A knife used by a fisherman will be far different from one used by a backpacker. The quality of steel and its ability to hold an edge are major concerns. A backpacker who carries a large hunting knife, machete, or hatchet is as over-equipped as a fly fisherman who carries a few sticks of dynamite to his favorite fishing hole.

A simple knife with two folding blades is functional and adequate for most wilderness uses. Some folding knives have a variety of equipment attached. You can find knives with saws, scissors, toothpicks, screw drivers, and corkscrews attached. Although some backpackers may find use for packing a double-bitted axe or chainsaw into the woods, a more modest and appropriate tool is a simple, quality double-bladed knife.

Backpackers, boaters, and those who venture into remote areas with their motor vehicles need survival kits. A survival kit will depend upon one's own personal needs and the method of travel. A kit is personal, in that medicine and other personal requirements will vary. Therefore, all survival kits may have some common items but they will also be different. Three principles must be kept in mind, however: All kits should be practical, all items must be essential, and all must be compact.

In almost all cases, a survival kit, no matter what its purpose, includes the following essentials. First and most important, matches, including at least some in a waterproof container. A candle, also essential, can be used to assist in fire-starting, but also for light, sterilization, and other purposes. A small, quality pocket knife is always needed. A map and compass are also essential for most trips. The scale of the map may vary but should include enough detail to enable you to locate major landmarks, sources of water, and cabins or ranger stations. A flashlight is essential. Its size is not important as long as it is in good working order and has spare dependable batteries. A first-aid kit is also essential. Its contents should include any personal medicines that may be needed. It should have at least one large triangular bandage, a few smaller bandages, water purification tablets or iodine. Carry salt tablets in desert country. A small needle and thread can be used to sew up major wounds in an emergency. Depending on anticipated conditions, a survival kit should include extra food and water. Concentrated foods like beef jerky, candy, granola, and gorp (a mixture of nuts, seeds, and dried fruit) should be carefully stored. Small, compact, but nutritious foods with a long storage life are important. Bouillon cubes, dried soup mixes, and other such items, although their salt content is high, can be used as a base for a soup or stew. Other natural and wild food items can supplement them.

In desert areas, sunglasses are essential. Those who wear corrective lenses may want to carry a spare pair of glasses, especially a pair with plastic lenses. A small compact waterproof pen will be useful for leaving messages, taking notes, and perhaps keeping a journal of wilderness experiences.

13

Survival of the Wilderness

Wilderness — the word is mystical. Images stir in the mind at the sound. Memories flow to far-off mountains, cool woods, or green, flowering meadows. The cry of a loon, the raucous sound of a sandhill crane, or the howl of a coyote stirs a primitive vision. Wilderness can trigger more memories, scenes, and senses than almost any other word. It belongs to everyone, but it is also a unique perception.

Wilderness is controversial — important to some, repugnant to others. At times the debate seems pointless, because for every acre protected as wilderness, at least four acres, now under asphalt and concrete, are allocated to machines, automobiles, and trucks. Parks and wilderness constitute a small fraction of what was once a wild, undeveloped continent.

Wilderness as a controversy is complex. For some, wilderness is the opposite of what the nation stands for — progress, development, and growth. For them, it represents stagnation or, worse, the pagan worship of nature. But for others, wilderness is not only part of our history and heritage but also the last and only frontier we will know.

Although it is not essential for an individual to learn wilderness survival, it is imperative that a nation assure the survival of wilderness. For, like fertile soils, clean air and water, wilderness as a natural resource contributes to national strength, vitality, and well-being. Collective wilderness skills and survival expertise likewise serve the national interest. Wilderness furnishes the experience through which self-reliance and independence are developed among a nation's citizens.

"In wildness is the preservation of the world," declared Henry David Thoreau in April 1854 — and the movement to conserve wilderness was launched. Later, John Muir widely publicized the message in his books and articles. Muir tramped the mountains, founded the Sierra Club, and left his indelible mark on wilderness conservation. Many years later, the words of Thoreau and Muir and the wilderness itself inspired Bob Marshall, Aldo Leopold, Sigurd Olson, Olaus and Adolph Murie and other conservation activists to work for wilderness preservation. Gradually, wildland was protected in parks, wildlife refuges, and forests. After a decade of effort, the Wilderness Act was finally passed in 1964, establishing a system of lands forever wild.

Where wilderness has been preserved — in deserts, swamps, and on the grasslands of the Great Plains — images of history can be relived in the mind: fur trappers and voyagers crossing lakes in Minnesota and Ontario; the Lewis and Clark expedition pulling up the Missouri River in Montana; gold seekers struggling over the Sierras into California.

In his 1893 essay, "The Significance of the Frontier in American History," Frederick Jackson Turner insisted that the frontier was a major force in the evolution of America and of Western democracy. According to Turner, Americans and their institutions were shaped by the frontier, and an understanding of the frontier was essential to appreciating American history. Few other nations have had a similar frontier, and without it, wrote Turner, other nations have been less innovative, less idealistic, less independent. The frontier stimulated lawlessness and violent solutions to problems, but also ingenuity and independence.

Turner noted that the passing of the frontier was depriving the nation of a significant factor in its evolution. Those who worked to protect wilderness and parkland from encroachment and development helped to establish a tangible alternative to the original frontier and helped also to assure an important institution for wilderness education. With wilderness and parkland conservation, the frontier experience has not been entirely lost, and indeed for many it can still bring a challenge. The frontier dream has been a powerful historical symbol, and conservationists have assured that it will continue in the wilderness.

Wilderness viewed as a symbol of the American frontier helps to explain the support and sympathy that wilderness preservation has received. A wilderness frontier cannot be the same as the old frontier in magnitude, but it can be similar in its influence on the individual. It means more in its natural state than in terms of the timber, minerals, and other tangible resources it may hold.

As the frontier receded to the west and most of the wilderness resources were exploited and wasted, the meaning of wilderness changed, for most people, from a hostile area to fear and subdue (as in the Bible) to a land of promise and peace. And as the nation began to urbanize, wilderness became a sanctuary, a place of hope and dreams.

Now that urban areas and development are so widespread, wilderness is needed, not as an alternative, but as a contrast and complement to civilization. Massive environmental changes make it as essential to preserve remnants of the frontier as to preserve a historic site or historic documents like the Declaration of Independence. Indeed, William O. Douglas advocated a wilderness bill of rights guaranteeing the existence of wilderness as fundamental to democracy as freedom of speech or of religious expression.

In *A Sand County Almanac,* Aldo Leopold gives three important reasons — recreation, science, and wildlife — for preserving the wilderness. Of these, recreation is both a popular and practical reason. Many millions of backpackers who take to the wildlands each year seek a physical challenge, an escape from urban life. Scouts learn camping crafts and an increased sense of self-reliance and self-worth. Through wilderness activities, many people experience non-economic, even spiritual values, and others develop an appreciation of the pioneers and their survival skills.

Wilderness provides a natural scientific benchmark for measuring environmental change. Ecologists and biologists often study the natural landscape for comparison with complex biological changes elsewhere. As the rest of the world becomes increasingly developed, the research rationale for wilderness becomes even more important.

Some people support wilderness because it is essential habitat for certain species as well as for the survival of the grizzly bear, and other species, and because protection benefits elk, mountain lions, and various other animals. However, many wildlife management agencies oppose wilderness because they are prohibited from altering the environment to increase the numbers of game animals.

Aldo Leopold's reasons for preserving wilderness are still valid today. In addition, wilderness has widespread support as an idea, a cultural symbol like the eagle — wild, untamed, and free. It strikes receptive feelings and images which are also expressed in art, poetry, and literature. Many regard it as a heritage to pass on to the next generation.

Nearly one hundred years after the closing of the great frontier, wilderness provides an environment in which personal change is still possible. Like frontier experiences, the wilderness experience represents an opportunity to better one's physical and psychic condition. The endowment of wilderness therapy lasts throughout the life of an individual.

As on the frontier, individuals who are spiritually limited by the urban environment can escape from their frustrations and restrictions, can rediscover the joy of fresh air, miles of travel on foot, acquiring a naturally tired body, and a sky bright with stars.

In the wilderness, time and life are put into a wild perspective. Humans and their artifacts are not dominant. The experience is humbling but can also foster a sense of independence. The desperate activity of the ordinary world diminishes, and we are calmed. By increasing our self-reliance, wilderness gives us not only respect for the land, but respect for our own lives. As personal esteem in enhanced, so also is the concept of responsibility. Travel in the wilderness decreases our dependence upon others in emergencies as well as in daily life. Collectively, this increased self-reliance can enhance our community. The wilderness experience can help us value ourselves in a crowded, impersonal world. For the freedom of wilderness travels with each individual even after he leaves.

Status and power mean nothing in the wilderness. The rain and wind affect all hikers the same, regardless of social or economic status. The water is equally cold; the sense of darkness is foreboding for everyone. The poorest student and the wealthiest banker may share a common trail or campsite. In a crisis, they are only as equal as the ingenuity and determination they can find in themselves. More than a hundred years ago, after hardship and pain, travelers on the Oregon Trail surely experienced a similar sense of equality.

Throughout the world, wildlands are continually lost to logging, mining, and overgrazing. But wilderness travelers learn to accept and respect the land. The essentials of life are put into perspective. Oxygen, clean water, nutritious food, and simple shelters provide the basics of existence.

Fortunately, we have not given up all our lands to development. To do so would be to surrender the opportunity for many wilderness experiences. Without wilderness and parkland, an important element of human life, the opportunity for a test against nature, would be lost. Even a chance encounter with injury or death can be important, for wilderness presents not security but the opportunity to learn from nature and to grow and develop as an individual.

In wilderness and parklands it is still possible to develop the confidence and vitality that Frederick Jackson Turner felt were essential to democracy. Today, as part of their wilderness experience, people are encouraged to invent, to substitute, and to be creative. They can still sense a pioneering spiritual dimension in the wilderness and the emotional enrichment it provides.

But wilderness cannot be protected in a vacuum. Conservation organizations and dedicated individuals write letters, work, and organize for the protection of parks and wildlands that generate oxygen to purify air polluted by the modern world and for the preservation of plant and animal species. Although many of them may never actually visit wild areas, they recognize the vitality of the natural world and they understand the importance of wildland preservation to the nation and to themselves. Wilderness becomes their link between the past and the future. Those who value the wilderness have a special responsibility to help protect the land for future generations. As long as they recognize the importance of wilderness conservation, the challenge of survival will be assured.

Selected Bibliography

GENERAL REFERENCES

Acerrano, Anthony J: *The Outdoorman's Emergency Manual.* New York: Winchester, 1976. A sportsman's survival manual.

Angier, Bradford. *Survival with Style.* Harrisburg, Pa.: Stackpole, 1972. An overview of survival from a sportsman's view.

Berglund, Berndt. *Wilderness Survival.* New York: Scribner, 1974. Well-illustrated and comprehensive.

Craighead, Frank C., Jr., and John J. Craighead. *How to Survive on Land and Sea: Individual Survival.* Annapolis, Md.: U.S. Naval Institute, 1958. The standard survival manual for many years, world-wide in coverage.

Nesbitt, Paul H., Alonzo W. Pond, and William H. Allen. *The Survival Book.* New York: Funk & Wagnalls, 1968. Based on military survival manuals and global in coverage.

Olsen, Larry Dean. *Outdoor Survival Skills.* Provo, Utah: Brigham Young University Press, 1973. The best single book on Indian-type survival skills.

Stefansson, Vilhjalmur. *Arctic Manual.* New York: Macmillan, 1944. A classic Arctic survival manual, complete with a description of how to handle dirigibles in the north.

Troebst, Cord Christian. *The Art of Survival*. Garden City, N.Y.: Doubleday, 1965. Translated from German and full of survival stories from around the world.

U.S. Department of the Air Force. *Search and Rescue Survival*. Washington, D.C.: U.S. Government Printing Office, 1969. The basic military survival manual, global in scope.

SURVIVAL ATTITUDE

Bickel, Lennard. *Mawson's Will*. New York: Avon, 1977. The story of Antarctic explorer Mawson is a classic example of the will to live.

Byrd, Richard E. *Alone*. New York: Putnam, 1938. Byrd's account of being isolated during an Antarctic winter has useful insights into survival attitudes.

Fear, Gene. *Surviving the Unexpected Wilderness Emergency*. Tacoma, Wash.: Survival Education Association, 1972. A general survival book with some useful points on the will to live.

Lansing, Alfred. *Endurance*. New York: Avon, 1960. Probably the finest example of the determination to survive — Shackleton's expedition to the Antarctic.

McGlashan, C. F. *History of the Donner Party: A Tragedy of the Sierra*. Stanford, Calif: Stanford University Press, 1947. An early account of the many problems of the Donner party.

Read, Piers Paul. *Alive: The Story of the Andes Survivors*. Philadelphia & New York: Lippincott, 1974. A fascinating tale of survival.

Stewart, George R. *Ordeal by Hunger: The Classic Story of the Donner Party*. New York: Pocket Books, 1971. A classic tale of cannibalism and survival.

Todd, A. L. *Abandoned*. New York: McGraw-Hill, 1961. A gruesome tale of the Greeley expedition to the Arctic.

SHELTERS

Gallagher, J. Q. "Survival — Physiologic and Psychologic Aspects." *Rocky Mountain Medical Journal*, October 1969. A discussion of the medical aspects of survival.

Kenton, Edith. *Protective Clothing: Arctic and Tropical Environments*. Springfield, Va.: National Technical Information Service, 1979. A complete bibliography with abstracts on clothing for environmental protection.

Kephart, Horace. *Camping and Woodcraft*. New York: Macmillan, 1921. An old guide to wilderness shelters.

Rutstrum, Calvin. *Paradise Below Zero*. New York: Macmillan, 1968. Basically a collection of stories from the far north with some good survival examples.

HYPOTHERMIA

Chinard, F. P. "Accidental Hypothermia — a Brief Review." *Journal of the Medical Society of New Jersey.* August 1978. An overview of the problem.

Harrison, Elizabeth A. *Cold Weather Stress on Humans.* Springfield, Va.: National Technical Information Service, 1977. Selected abstracts on cold stress.

Lathrop, Theodore G. *Hypothermia: Killer of the Unprepared.* Portland, Ore.: Mazamas, 1972. The best single explanation of hypothermia.

Pugh, L. G. "Accidental Hypothermia in Walkers, Climbers, and Campers." *British Medical Journal,* January 1966. An early article on hypothermia.

FIRE

Fire is discussed in the general survival books. An especially good discussion is found in Olsen, Larry Dean. *Outdoor Survival Skills.* Provo, Utah: Brigham Young University Press, 1973.

U.S. Forest Service. *Fireman's Handbook.* Washington, D.C.: U.S. Government Printing Office, 1966.

WATER

Allen, William H. "Thirst." *Natural History,* October 1956. An easy-to-read article on a complex subject.

Jackson, Ray D., and C. H. M. Van Bavel. "Solar Distillation of Water from Soil and Plant Materials: A Simple Desert Survival Technique." *Science,* September 17, 1965. A technical article on a solar still.

Kahn, Fredrick H., and Barbara R. Visscher. "Water Disinfection in the Wilderness." *Summit,* April-May, 1977. A simple method of water purification.

Wolf, A. V. *Thirst: Physiology of the Urge to Drink and Problems of Water Lack.* Springfield, Ill.: Thomas, 1958. A complete technical discussion of thirst.

FOOD

Angier, Bradford. *Free for the Eating.* Harrisburg, Pa.: Stackpole, 1966. One of the many guides to edible plants.

Burt, William Henry, and Richard Philip Grossenheider. *A Field Guide to the Mammals.* Boston: Houghton Mifflin, 1964. One of the excellent Peterson Field Guide books.

Coon, Nelson. *The Dictionary of Useful Plants.* Emmaus, Pa.: Rodale, 1974. An excellent source of information.

Craighead, John J., Frank C. Craighead, Jr., and Ray J. Davis. *A Field*

Guide to Rocky Mountain Wildflowers. Boston: Houghton Mifflin, 1963. Also a Peterson guide, fundamental and excellent.

Gibbons, Euell. *Stalking the Healthful Herbs.* New York: McKay, 1970. This and other books by Gibbons are very good.

Gibbons, Euell. *Stalking the Wild Asparagus.* New York: McKay, 1962. More edible plant lore from Euell Gibbons.

Harrington, H. D. *Western Edible Wild Plants.* Albuquerque, N.M.: The University of New Mexico Press, 1972. Well-illustrated guide to western plants.

Kirk, Donald R. *Wild Edible Plants of the Western United States.* Healdsburg, Calif.: Naturegraph Publishers, 1970. One of the many edible food guide books.

Medsger, Oliver Perry. *Edible Wild Plants.* New York: Collier, 1974. A reprint of a classic edible plant book.

Muenscher, Walter Conrad. *Poisonous Plants of the United States.* New York: Collier, 1975. A comprehensive look at poisonous plants.

Murie, Olaus J. *A Field Guild to Animal Tracks.* Boston: Houghton Mifflin, 1954. A fascinating guide to animal tracks by a famous conservationist.

Tampion, John. *Dangerous Plants.* New York: Universe, 1977. A well-illustrated guide.

Weiner, Michael A. *Earth Medicine – Earth Foods.* New York: Collier, 1974. Medicinal plants and Indian lore.

Wheat, Margaret M. *Survival Arts of the Primitive Paiutes.* Reno, Nev.: University of Nevada Press, 1967. A wonderful guide to Indian survival skills.

TRAVEL AND ROUTEFINDING

Disley, John. *Orienteering.* Harrisburg, Pa.: Stackpole, 1973. An excellent introduction to the sport of orienteering.

Gatty, Harold. *Nature Is Your Guide: How to Find Your Way on Land and Sea.* New York: Penguin, 1979. The finest book available on using nature as a guide.

Kjellstrom, Bjorn. *Be Expert with Map and Compass: The Orienteering Handbook.* New York: Scribner, 1972. A good introduction to the use of maps and compass.

Rutstrum, Calvin. *The Wilderness Routefinder.* New York: Collier, 1973. An excellent introduction to routefinding.

Vines, Tom. "Lost!" *Outdoor Life*, February 1980. A good discussion of how to locate someone lost in the woods.

WEATHER

Anthes, Richard A., Hans A. Panosky, John J. Cahir, and Albert

Rango. *The Atmosphere*. Columbus, Ohio: Merrill, 1978. A standard college textbook on meteorology.

Battan, Louis J. *Nature of Violent Storms*. New York: Doubleday, 1961. Basic discussion of thunderstorms, hurricanes, and tornadoes.

Edinger, J. G. *Watching for the Wind*. New York: Doubleday, 1967. An enjoyable book stressing local meteorology.

Frazier, Kendrick. *The Violent Face of Weather*. New York: Morrow, 1979. Explanation and case studies of natural disasters.

Lehr, Paul E., R. Will Burnett, and Herbert S. Zim. *Weather*. New York: Golden Press, 1965. A well-illustrated, simple introduction for the novice.

Sloane, Eric. *Folklore of American Weather*. New York: Meredith, 1963. A small but useful collection of weather proverbs with an explanation.

DESERT SURVIVAL

Adolph, E. F., et al. *Physiology of Man in the Desert*. New York: Interscience, 1947. A classic study of desert survival.

Arnold, Robert E. *What to Do About Bites and Stings of Venomous Animals*. New York: Macmillan, 1973. A first-aid book for desert country.

Dunbier, Roger. *The Sonoran Desert*. Tucson, Ariz.: University of Arizona Press, 1968. History, geography, and natural history of the Sonoran Desert.

George, Uwe. *In the Deserts of This Earth*. New York: Harcourt Brace Jovanovich, 1977. An overview of the world's deserts and adaptations of man and animals to them.

Jaeger, Edmund C. *The North American Deserts*. Palo Alto, Calif.: Stanford University Press, 1957. A standard work on American deserts and their natural history.

Krutch, Joseph Wood. *The Desert Year*. New York: Sloane, 1961. An evocative look at deserts. This and Krutch's other books on desert country are excellent.

Larson, Peggy. *The Deserts of the Southwest*. San Francisco: Sierra Club, 1977. One of the best guides to the natural history of the Southwest deserts, including survival and plants useful in finding water.

Stebbins, Robert C. *A Field Guide to Western Reptiles and Amphibians*. Boston: Houghton Mifflin, 1975. A standard work on the natural history of reptiles and amphibians.

MOUNTAIN SURVIVAL

Brower, David. *Manual of Ski Mountaineering*. San Francisco: Sierra

Club, 1962. A classic winter survival book by a foremost defender of wilderness.

Clarke, Charles, Michael Ward, and Edward Williams. *Mountain Medicine and Physiology*. London: Alpine Club, 1975. Technical discussion of mountain physiology.

Craighead, Frank C., Jr. *Track of the Grizzly*. San Francisco: Sierra Club, 1979. The best book on the natural history of grizzlies.

Ferber, P. (ed.). *Mountaineering: The Freedom of the Hills*. Seattle: The Mountaineers, 1975. The best single book on mountaineering.

Hock, Raymond J. "The Physiology of High Altitude." *Scientific American*, February 1970. Helpful in understanding the effects of altitude.

Jerome, John. *On Mountains: Thinking About Terrain*. New York: McGraw-Hill, 1978. A comprehensive look at mountains.

Martinelli, M., Jr. *Snow Avalanche Sites*. (Agriculture Information Bulletin 360.) Washington, D.C.: U.S. Government Printing Office, February 1974. How to identify avalance sites.

Perla, Ronald I., and M. Martinelli, Jr. *Avalanche Handbook*. (Agriculture Handbook 489.) Washington, D.C.: U.S. Government Printing Office, 1976. The best technical discussion on avalanches.

Wilkerson, James A. *Medicine for Mountaineering*. Seattle: The Mountaineers, 1967. An excellent source of information on mountain first aid and survival.

SEA SURVIVAL

Heyerdahl, Thor. *Kon-Tiki: Across the Pacific by Raft*. Chicago: Rand McNally, 1950. A fascinating story about sea survival.

Lee, Eric, and Kenneth Lee. *Safety and Survival at Sea*. New York: Norton, 1971. One of the best sea survival books.

National Science Foundation. *Survival in Antarctica*. Washington, D.C.: U.S. Government Printing Office, 1979. Excellent on the Antarctic, including sea survival.

Robertson, Dougal. *Sea Survival: A Manual*. New York: Praeger, 1975. A complete sea survival manual.

Wade, Wyn Craig. *The Titanic: End of a Dream*. New York: Rawson, Wade, 1979. A recent book on the *Titanic* disaster.

PREPARATION

Bridge, Raymond. *America's Backpacking Book*. New York: Scribner, 1973. A basic introduction to backpacking.

Bridge, Raymond. *The Complete Snow Camper's Guide*. New York: Scribner, 1973. A good introduction to winter camping.

Explorers Ltd. (ed.). *The Explorers Ltd. Source Book*. New York: Harper and Row, 1977. A fascinating collection of information for the outdoor person.

Fletcher, Colin. *The Complete Walker*. New York: Knopf, 1973. A well-written and opinionated book on hiking. A delight.

Kemsley, William, Jr. (ed.). *Backpacking Equipment*. New York: Collier, 1975. The best single source book on determining quality backpacking equipment.

Langer, Richard W. *The Joy of Camping*. Baltimore, Md.: Penguin, 1974. A comprehensive look at camping.

SURVIVAL OF THE WILDERNESS

Abbey, Edward. *Desert Solitaire*. New York: McGraw-Hill, 1968. This and other books and articles by Abbey are well-written defenses of wilderness.

Brooks, Paul. *Roadless Area*. New York: Ballantine, 1971. A fine collection of articles on wildlands.

Gilliam, Ann (ed.). *Voices for the Earth: A Treasury of the Sierra Club Bulletin*. San Francisco: Sierra Club, 1979. An excellent collection of articles.

Graber, Linda H. *Wilderness as Sacred Space*. Washington, D.C.: Association of American Geographers, 1976. A little-known but excellent analysis of wilderness in modern life.

Leopold, Aldo. *A Sand County Almanac*. New York: Oxford University Press, 1949. An enduring classic on wilderness and nature.

Nash, Roderick. *Wilderness and the American Mind*. New Haven: Yale University Press, 1967. A scholarly analysis of wilderness in North America.

Major National
Wilderness Conservation Organizations

Although it is impossible to list all the many excellent statewide and local organizations devoted to the conservation of wilderness, some of the major national organizations are listed below.

American Hiking Society
317 Pennsylvania Avenue, S.E.
Washington, DC 20003

A new organization concerned with hiking and trails.

American Rivers Conservation
Council
317 Pennsylvania Avenue, S.E.
Washington, DC 20003

An excellent organization working to conserve free-flowing rivers.

Appalachian Mountain Club
5 Joy Street
Boston, MA 02108

An organization providing backcountry education and service in the Northeast.

American Wilderness Alliance
4260 East Evans Avenue, #8
Denver, CO 80222

A recently formed organization highly effective because of a dedicated and experienced staff and its concentration on wilderness issues.

Friends of the Earth
124 Spear Street
San Francisco, CA 94105

A worldwide conservation group concerned with the rational use of the earth.

National Audubon Society
950 Third Avenue
New York, NY 10022

One of the oldest and largest conservation organizations in North America.

National Parks and
Conservation Association
1701 18th Street, N.W.
Washington, DC 20009

Devoted to the conservation of national parks and monuments.

Public Lands Institute
1740 High Street
Denver, CO 80218

Another new organization devoted to the conservation of public lands.

Sierra Club
530 Bush Street
San Francisco, CA 94108

Founded by John Muir and long regarded as one of the most effective conservation groups.

The Wilderness Society
1901 Pennsylvania Ave., N.W.
Washington, DC 20006

The oldest wilderness organization now advocating a North American land ethic.

Index